AF510504

Lectures in Production and Supply

World Scientific Lecture Notes in Economics and Policy

ISSN: 2630-4872

The World Scientific Lecture Notes in Economics and Policy series is aimed to produce lecture note texts for a wide range of economics disciplines, both theoretical and applied at the undergraduate and graduate levels. Contributors to the series are highly ranked and experienced professors of economics who see in publication of their lectures a mission to disseminate the teaching of economics in an affordable manner to students and other readers interested in enriching their knowledge of economic topics. The series was formerly titled World Scientific Lecture Notes in Economics.

Published:

Vol. 23: *Lectures in Production and Supply*
by Barry K. Goodwin

Vol. 22: *Lectures on Probability and Statistics for Graduate-Level Economics*
by Antonio Jiménez-Martínez

Vol. 21: *Lecture Notes in Experimental Economics*
by John Duff

Vol. 20: *Public Policy and Climate Change: Politics, Philosophy and Economics*
by John Quiggin

For the complete list of volumes in this series, please visit
www.worldscientific.com/series/wslnep

World Scientific Lecture Notes in Economics and Policy – Vol. 23

Lectures in Production and Supply

Barry K. Goodwin
North Carolina State University, USA

World Scientific

NEW JERSEY • LONDON • SINGAPORE • BEIJING • SHANGHAI • HONG KONG • TAIPEI • CHENNAI • TOKYO

Published by

World Scientific Publishing Co. Pte. Ltd.
5 Toh Tuck Link, Singapore 596224
USA office: 27 Warren Street, Suite 401-402, Hackensack, NJ 07601
UK office: 57 Shelton Street, Covent Garden, London WC2H 9HE

British Library Cataloguing-in-Publication Data
A catalogue record for this book is available from the British Library.

World Scientific Lecture Notes in Economics and Policy — Vol. 23
LECTURES IN PRODUCTION AND SUPPLY

ISBN 9789811298264 (hardcover)
ISBN 9789819800230 (paperback)
ISBN 9789811298271 (ebook for institutions)
ISBN 9789811298288 (ebook for individuals)

For any available supplementary material, please visit
https://www.worldscientific.com/worldscibooks/10.1142/13986#t=suppl

Desk Editor: Jiang Yulin

Typeset by Stallion Press
Email: enquiries@stallionpress.com

Contents

Foreword to

ECG741 "Production and Supply Economics" Notes

This set of notes has formed the basis of my doctoral production economics class at North Carolina State University (NCSU). This class is one of a two-class sequence that comprises the agricultural economics field in the economics graduate program at NCSU. Doctoral students in the economics program select two or three fields of specialization as a portion of their training for a Ph.D. degree in Economics. I have taught this class approximately 15 times over the twenty-year period between 2003–2023. The other field class focuses on consumer demand and markets. These notes should be used in conjunction with the included course outline. The course necessarily builds off of readings in the contemporary literature. This material will quickly become dated and anyone using these notes should be cautioned to continually update the materials to keep pace with an evolving professional literature.

The class focuses on topics in production and supply. A central focus of the course addresses contemporary agricultural policy issues. In recent years, agricultural insurance and risk analysis have been important policy issues and have been a central focus of much of the course. Topics in risk analysis include density estimation, nonparametric analysis, and multivariate analysis using copulas.

It is essential to emphasize that the central core of production economics used in this course is drawn from the excellent text of Robert Chambers, *Applied Production Analysis*. My notes necessarily duplicate (and explicitly copy in many instances) much of the material in Bob's outstanding text. I have consulted with Bob to make clear the publisher's intent to publish my notes and, by extension, to repeat much of the material in his text and I believe I have his blessing. I want to emphasize to avoid any misunderstanding — *much of the material contained in my lecture notes is drawn directly from Bob Chamber's excellent textbook.* Whether this constitutes a case of drive-by plagiarism, I will let others decide. However, anyone utilizing this material should understand that a more thorough and superior treatment of the material is contained in Bob's text. The material is not mine and I claim no originality in my treatment of the subject.

Two of my outstanding graduate students — Jaimie Choi and Jack Robinson — performed all of the editing of this material. I am, of course, responsible for any errors that remain. I cannot thank Jaimie and Jack enough and their contribution to this project is immense. Thank you, Jaimie and Jack!

ECG 741

Agricultural Production and Supply

North Carolina State University

Fall 2021

Barry K. Goodwin
4221-C Nelson Hall
(919) 515-4620
E-mail: barry_goodwin@ncsu.edu

Class Hours: Tuesday and Thursday, 11:45-1:00

Class Location: Online

Office Hours: Via Zoom Tuesday and Thursday, 2:00–3:00 p.m. and by *advance appointment*. You *must* alert me in advance if you want to meet. I will try to always be available during these office hours, but it works best if you drop me a note in advance. I am very flexible on meeting with you. This includes evening meetings if necessary. I hope to be on campus on Mondays and you are welcome to drop by my office without advanced notice. However, depending on how the semester goes, it will still be optimal to drop a note in advance as this might save you a wasted trip.

I will always attempt to be available during these times, though there will be a few occasions when I have obligations that pull me away during office hours. I will attempt to notify you in advance of any such occasions. Though I do not anticipate it, travel could take me away from campus for a short period of time. We will schedule makeup sessions if needed later in the semester.

In-Person Meetings: I hope to schedule frequent in-person class meetings. We can discuss this, but I propose Monday afternoons. I will arrange a room and we will attempt to set a time that does not conflict with your other obligations or seminars.

E-mail is the most efficient means of communication and I will use it extensively in the class. You must check your mail daily.

Class Website: We will utilize the NCSU ClassTech 'Moodle' website, which is accessible through http://moodle.wolfware.ncsu.edu.

Optional (*Highly Recommended*) Text:
Chambers, Robert G., *Applied Production Analysis: A Dual Approach*, New York: Cambridge University Press, 1988.

Optional:
Goodwin, B. K., J. Chvosta, and F. Ramsey. *Applied Econometrics with SAS: Modeling Demand, Supply, and Risk*, SAS Institute; 1 edition (March 22, 2018).

The first text is an excellent (though increasingly dated) book that presents an overview of applied production analysis. Much of the material should have already been covered in the core micro courses and will not be repeated here, with the possible exception of a few quick reviews. Thus, you will be fine without purchasing the text. Having said this, this text would be an excellent addition to your professional library. The second book contains examples, many of which were based on class assignments. We will work through much of this in class. I do not recommend that you buy/borrow this as I will give you the necessary coding.

We will mainly rely upon readings from the professional literature, as identified on the attached reading list. You are responsible for reading each paper *prior* to its discussion in class. Though we will not follow a rigid schedule, if you are at all engaged in the class, you will know exactly what to read in advance of the lectures.

Course Objectives and Overview:

This is a class in the applied analysis of issues pertinent to the production and supply of agricultural commodities. We will take a broad approach to this general area of inquiry and we will consider issues in the following areas: production and cost conditions, factor demand relationships, the adoption of technology, technical change, quality and damage control, models of risk and insurance, and current issues in agricultural policy. Our approach will be focused on applied *empirical* analysis. I will assume complete familiarity with issues pertinent to production costs and supply that were covered in the micro core theory courses as well as with econometric issues associated with the estimation of systems of equations and maximum likelihood methods. You must be familiar with this material at the level of coverage offered in the core theory and econometrics classes.

Homework Assignments:

The class will include a number of homework assignments (I anticipate approximately 6 assignments). These assignments will mainly consist of exercises involving empirical estimation. SAS will be our main tool for conducting these analyses, though I will also utilize the R language throughout the semester. R is a standard in statistics and in other disciplines and has substantial advantages in that it is extremely flexible, freely available, widely-used, and relatively fast. In addition, R has a very wide community of users with many add-on packages. I will provide you with a number of help resources on R. You can access the main repository for R at http://www.r-project.org/. You are, of course, welcome to do your analysis in any software of your choice. The university has site licenses to MATLAB, LIMDEP, TSP, and many other packages. If you choose to use another such package, I may not be able to help you as much with coding issues.

Research Paper:

The most important part of the class is the research paper. It comprises the largest, single component of your final grade. Further, writing papers of this sort will probably be one of the most important activities of your career. Ideally, you should view this as an opportunity to define a dissertation topic. Many students write papers that end up forming a chapter in their dissertation. You should plan on writing a paper that can be presented at a professional meeting and/or submitted for publication in an academic journal. I have had many students realize success in eventually publishing their field course papers and this should be a goal for everyone. A few guidelines for the paper:

1. A premium will be placed on *originality*.
2. You will not receive full credit for a paper that has been or will be submitted to fulfill the obligations of another course or other academic requirements, either here at NCSU or at another institution. For example, a paper lifted from your masters' thesis will not receive full credit.
3. The papers will be due on the last regular day of class, with *no* exceptions.
4. The topic of your paper is your choice — as long as it pertains to some theoretical or empirical issue relating to the economics of production, supply, policy, or any other topic of relevance to the course material.
5. You should feel free to submit ideas and outlines to me for your paper. This is not a requirement, but I will give you as much help as possible if you alert me to your topic in advance.
6. I will only read your complete paper once, though I will be very pleased to discuss your progress at any time. I don't have the capacity to proofread papers in advance of the due date.
7. Everyone should plan to submit the paper for consideration to be presented at professional society meetings (e.g., the ASSA, AAEA, JSM, NCR-134, and Econometric Society meetings, etc.). There are many benefits to doing this (which we will discuss) and we are always well-represented by our students at such meetings.
8. We may consider oral presentations of your papers in lieu of a final exam. I have done this on occasion and find it to be good practice. We will discuss this well in advance of the final date. If we do this, the final exam portion of your grade will be determined by the quality of your paper and presentation.

Grading:

- Homework: 20%
- Midterm Exam: 20%
- Final Exam: 20%
- Research Paper: 40%

As noted, we have occasionally had presentations of the research papers as a final exam. I think everyone has enjoyed this and it is good practice for what you will likely be doing professionally. We will entertain this possibility as the time approaches.

Accommodations for Students with Disabilities:

Any student with a documented disability may request arrangements to accommodate their disability. Such arrangements include the provision of services and reasonable accommodations appropriate to the student's disability. This should be arranged through the DSS office. See the office website for more information. http://www.ncsu.edu/provost/offices/affirm-action/dss/

Academic Integrity:

Academic misconduct includes, but is not limited to: cheating, aiding and abetting others to cheat, destruction or removal of academic material without permission, and plagiarism (NCSU POL11.35.01). Every student is expected to be familiar with and to adhere to the North Carolina State University Code of Student Conduct. This can be found at http://www2.ncsu.edu/ncsu/stud-affairs/policies/code95.html

Uploading of student notes or other course documents to external websites or apps that encourage students to share course information is a violation of NC State's copyright regulation. Notes of classroom and laboratory lectures and exercises taken by students shall not be deemed Student Works, may only be used for personal educational purposes, and cannot be used for commercialization by the student generating such notes or by any third party (NCSU REG 01.25.03).

Students who commit academic misconduct or violate the copyright regulation will be referred to the Office of Student Conduct. Violations of academic integrity will be handled in accordance with the Student Discipline Procedures (NCSU REG 11.35.02).

Community Standards Related to COVID-19

We are all responsible for protecting ourselves and our community. Please see the community expectations (NCSU Community Standards) and Rule 04.21.01 regarding Personal Safety Requirements Related to COVID-19 https://policies.ncsu.edu/rule/rul-04-21-01

A few final comments:

- I am thrilled to have the opportunity to teach this class. However, I must acknowledge that the material follows my own set of interests — there is no way that all relevant topics could be covered in a single semester course and thus you will get a sampling of the issues that I believe to be most important and/or interesting. If necessary, we will adjust the syllabus as the semester progresses to ensure that we cover the most critical materials.
- My research and teaching obligations may take me away from NCSU and may entail the need to reschedule a class session. This will be avoided if at all possible. I will want to make up any classes missed by holding a Friday afternoon meeting.
- Attendance at the departmental Agricultural Economics seminar series is a *mandatory* requirement of the course. The seminar series represents a homework assignment and will be graded accordingly.
- This class is listed as an in-person, lecture-style class. We will be conducting the class in a "hybrid" manner, meaning that we will utilize Zoom for lectures at least part of the time. We will see how this goes early on and will make adjustments as necessary.
- You should be aware of the fact that the graduate school has adopted a very strict policy about incomplete grades. Without going through the counseling center, you will likely not be able to request an incomplete. Keep this in mind as you consider the paper and other requirements of the course. Incomplete course grades will not be considered unless requested through the counseling center (i.e., indicating a significant issue that merits extending the grading period).
- Your field courses should be viewed as stepping stones into your dissertation research. You will be far ahead in the race if you emerge from this year with a firm dissertation topic in mind.

- The currency of academics is journal publications. In today's job market, most candidates already have some experience in this area (i.e., already have publications). I will emphasize this aspect of our profession throughout the semester — but plan now — think about presenting and publishing your work in every aspect of your training.

Course Outline and Assigned Readings*

I. Primal and Dual Theories of Production
   A. The Basic Problem
      Chambers — Chapters 1–2
      Chavas, Chambers, and Pope (2010)
      Mundlak (2001)*
      Pope (1982)
      Taylor (1989)
      Rosas and Lence (2019)
   B. Measures of Scale and Input Substitutability
      Chambers — Chapters 3–4
      Binswanger (1974)
   C. Flexibility in Empirical Models
      Chambers — Chapter 5 and 7
      LaFrance and Pope (2008)
      Plastina and Lence (2019)
      Kim (2005)
   D. Multiproduct Production Functions
      Just, Zilberman, and Hochman (1983)
      Just, Zilberman, Hochman, and Bar-Shira (1990)
      LaFrance and Pope (2010)
   E. Econometric Issues
      Diewert and Wales (1987)
      Geweke (1986)

Note that almost all of these readings are available online from JSTOR or from AgEcon Search (http://ageconsearch.umn.edu). Entries marked with a '#' are available through Elsevier's Science Direct while those marked with a '' are not available electronically and have thus been placed on reserve.

Ryan and Wales (1998)
Moschini and Moro (1994)

F. Nonparametric Modeling of Production
Chambers and Lichtenberg (1996)
Varian (1984)
O'Donnell (2012)

II. Producer Choice Under Uncertainty

A. The Basic Problem
Buschena and Zilberman (1994)
Sandmo (1971)
Moschini and Hennessy (2001)*
Lybbert and Just (2007)
Just and Peterson (2010)

B. Concepts of Insurance

C. Empirical Modeling of Crop Yield, Price, and Revenue Risks
Goodwin and Ker (2001)*
Goodwin and Ker (1998)
Ozaki, Ghosh, Goodwin, and Shirota (2008)

D. Crop Insurance
Goodwin (2001)
Goodwin (1994)
Goodwin (1993)
Keith H. Coble (2007)
Kuwayama, Thompson, Bernknopf, Zaitchik, and Vail (2019)
Ker and Tolhurst (2019)

E. Measuring Price Risk
Goodwin, Harri, Rejesus, and Coble (2018)
Ubilava (2018)

F. Copulas and Modeling Dependence
Mildenhall (2006)
Yan (2006)
Goodwin and Hungerford (2015)
Goodwin (2014)

III. Estimation of Risk Aversion Parameters
Bar-Shira, Just, and Zilberman (1997)
Roosen and Hennessy (2003)
Just and Just (2016)

IV. The Stochastic Specification of Empirical Models
Mundlak (1996)
Just and Pope (2001)*
Antle (1983)
Antle (1987)
Just and Pope (1979)
Just and Pope (1978)
Pope and Just (2003)
Pope and Just (2002)
Platoni, Sckokai, and Moro (2012)
Pope and Just (1996)♯
Moschini (2001)♯
Antle (1983)
Antle (1987)
Das, de Janvry, and Sadoulet (2019)
Chambers and Serra (2019)

V. Frontier Production Functions and Technical Efficiency
Battese (1992)
Kalirajan and Shand (1999)

VI. Self Protection, Quality, and Damage Control
Zilberman, Schmitz, Casterline, Lichtenberg, and Siebert (1991)
Chambers and Lichtenberg (1994)
Gertler and Waldman (1992)
Lichtenberg and Zilberman (1986)

VII. Asset Valuation
Goodwin, Mishra, and Ortalo-Magne (2003)
Kirwan (2009)
Goodwin, Mishra, and Ortalo-Magné (2012)♯

VIII. Technology
A. The Nature of Technology
Griliches (1957)
Olmstead and Rhode (1993)
B. The Adoption of New Technology
Goodwin and Piggott (2020)
Aldana, Foltz, Barham, and Useche (2011)
Liu and Shumway (2008)

Besley and Case (1993)
Feder (1980)
Feder, Just, and Zilberman (1985)
Feder and O'Mara (1981)
Feder and Slade (1984)
Griliches (1964)
Griliches (1958)
Kislev and Peterson (1981)
Hubbell, Marra, and Carlson (2000)

C. Learning by Doing and Technology Adoption
Jovanovic and Nyarko (1996)
Foster and Rosenzweig (1995)
Goodwin, Featherstone, and Zeuli (2002)

IX. Spatial Price Relationships
Fackler and Goodwin (2001)
Guney, Goodwin, and Riquelme (2018)

X. Structural Change
Chambers–Chapter 6
Chavas (2001)*
Goodwin and Brester (1995)
Morrison-Paul (1997)

XI. Time Allocation and Labor Supply

A. Off-Farm Labor Supply
Sumner (1982)
Huffman and Lange (1989)
Mishra and Goodwin (1997)

B. Endogenous Farm Structure
Ahituv and Kimhi (2002)♯
Kislev and Peterson (1982)

XII. Policy and Acreage Response Models

A. U.S. Agricultural Policy Background
Gardner (1992)
Gardner (1987)

B. Acreage Response Models
Gardner (1976)
Houck and Ryan (1972)

Chavas and Holt (1990)
Rucker, Thurman, and Sumner (1995)

C. Current Policy Issues
Kirwan, Uchida, and White (2012)
Hennessy (1998)
Goodwin and Mishra (2006)

Reading List

Ahituv, A., and A. Kimhi (2002): "Off-Farm Work and Capital Accumulation Decisions of Farmers," *Journal of Development Economics*, 68, 329–53.

Aldana, U., J. D. Foltz, B. L. Barham, and P. Useche (2011): "Sequential Adoption of Package Technologies: The Dynamics of Stacked Trait Corn Adoption," *American Journal Of Agricultural Economics*, 93, 130–143.

Antle, J. M. (1983): "Incorporating Risk in Production Analysis," *American Journal of Agricultural Economics*, 65, 1099–1106.

_______ (1987): "Econometric Estimation of Producers' Risk Attitudes," *American Journal of Agricultural Economics*, 69, 509–522.

Bar–Shira, Z., R. E. Just, and D. Zilberman (1997): "Estimation of farmers' Risk Attitude: An Econometric Approach," *Agricultural Economics*, 17(2–3), 211–222.

Battese, G. E. (1992): "Frontier Production Functions and Technical Efficiency: A Survey of Empirical Applications in Agricultural Economics," *Agricultural economics*, 7(3–4), 185–208.

Besley, T., and A. Case (1993): "Modeling Technology Adoption in Developing Countries," *American Economic Review*, 83, 396–402.

Binswanger, H. P. (1974): "A Cost Function Approach to the Measurement of Elasticities of Factor Demand and Elasticities of Substitution," *American Journal of Agricultural Economics*, 56, 377–86.

Buschena, D., and D. Zilberman (1994): "What Do We Know About Decision Making Under Risk And Where Do We Go From Here?," *Journal of Agricultural and Resource Economics*, 19, 425–444.

Chambers, R., and E. Lichtenberg (1994): "Simple Econometrics of Pesticide Productivity," *American Journal of Agricultural Economics*, 76, 407–417.

Chambers, R., and E. Lichtenberg (1996): "A Nonparametric Approach to von Liebig-Paris Technology," *American Journal of Agricultural Economics*, 78, 373–386.

Chambers, R. G., and T. Serra (2019): "Estimating Ex Ante Cost Functions for Stochastic Technologies," *American Journal of Agricultural Economics*, 101(3), 807–824.

Chavas, J. P. (2001): "Structural Change in Agricultural Production: Economics, Technology and Policy," in *Handbook of Agricultural Economics*, ed. by B. Gardner, and G. Rausser, vol. 1. North Holland, Amsterdam.

Chavas, J.-P., R. G. Chambers, and R. D. Pope (2010): "Production Economics and Farm Management: A Century of Contributions," *American Journal of Agricultural Economics*, 92(2), 356–375.

Chavas, J. P., and M. T. Holt (1990): "Acreage decisions under risk: The case of corn and soybeans," *American Journal of Agricultural Economics*, 72, 529–538.

Das, N., A. de Janvry, and E. Sadoulet (2019): "Credit and Land Contracting: A Test of the Theory of Sharecropping," *American Journal of Agricultural Economics*, 101(4), 1098–1114.

Diewert, W. E., and T. J. Wales (1987): "Flexible Functional Forms and Global Curvature Conditions," *Econometrica*, 55(1), 43–68.

Fackler, P. L., and B. K. Goodwin (2001): "Chapter 17 Spatial Price Analysis," *Handbook of Agricultural Economics*, 1, 971–1024, Marketing, Distribution and Consumers.

Feder, G. (1980): "Farm Size, Risk Aversion and the Adoption of New Technology under Uncertainty," *Oxford Economic Papers*, 32, 263–283.

Feder, G., R. F. Just, and D. Zilberman (1985): "Adoption of Agricultural Innovations in Developing Countries: A Survey," *Economic Development and Cultural Change*, 32, 225–298.

Feder, G., and G. T. O'Mara (1981): "Farm Size and the Diffusion of Green Revolution Technology," *Economic Development and Cultural Change*, 30, 59–76.

Feder, G., and R. Slade (1984): "The Acquisition of Information and the Adoption of New Technology," *American Journal of Agricultural Economics*, 66, 312–320.

Foster, A., and M. R. Rosenzweig (1995): "Learning by Doing and Learning from Others: Human Capital and Technical Change in Agriculture," *Journal of Political Economy*, 103, 1176–1209.

Gardner, B. (1992): "Changing Economic Perspectives on the Farm Problem," *Journal of Economic Literature*, 30, 62–101.

Gardner, B. L. (1976): "Futures Prices in Supply Analysis," *American Journal of Agricultural Economics*, 58, 81–84.

______ (1987): "Causes of US Farm Commodity Programs," *Journal of Political Economy*, 95, 290–310.

Gertler, P. J., and D. M. Waldman (1992): "Quality-adjusted Cost Functions and Policy Evaluation in the Nursing Home Industry," *Journal of Political Economy*, 100, 1232–1256.

Geweke, J. (1986): "Exact Inference in the Inequality Constrained Normal Linear Regression Model," *Journal of Applied Econometrics*, 1, 127–141.

Goodwin, B., and A. Ker (2001): "Modeling Price and Yield Risk," in *A Comprehensive Assessment of the Role of Risk in US Agriculture*, ed. by R. E. Just, and R. D. Pope, pp. 289–324. Kluwer Academic Publishers, Norwell, MA.

Goodwin, B. K. (1993): "An Empirical Analysis of the Demand for Multiple Peril Crop Insurance," *American Journal of Agricultural Economics*, 75(2), 425–434.

______ (1994): "Premium Rate Determination in the Federal Crop Insurance Program: What do Averages Have to Say About Risk?," *Journal of Agricultural and Resource Economics*, 382–395.

Goodwin, B. K. (2001): "Problems with Market Insurance in Agriculture," *American Journal Of Agricultural Economics*, 83(3), 643–649.

Goodwin, B. K. (2014): "Agricultural Policy Analysis: The Good, The Bad, and The Ugly," *American Journal of Agricultural Economics*, 97(2), 353–373.

Goodwin, B. K., and G. W. Brester (1995): "Structural-Change in Factor Demand Relationships in the United-States Food and Kindred Products Industry," *American Journal Of Agricultural Economics*, 77(1), 69–79.

Goodwin, B. K., A. M. Featherstone, and K. Zeuli (2002): "Producer Experience, Learning by Doing, and Yield Performance," *American Journal of Agricultural Economics*, 84(3), 660–678.

Goodwin, B. K., A. Harri, R. M. Rejesus, and K. H. Coble (2018): "Measuring Price Risk in Rating Revenue Coverage: BS or No BS?," *American Journal of Agricultural Economics*, 100(2), 456–478.

Goodwin, B. K., and A. Hungerford (2015): "Copula-Based Models of Systemic Risk in U.S. Agriculture: Implications for Crop Insurance and Reinsurance Contracts," *American Journal of Agricultural Economics*, 97(3), 879–896.

Goodwin, B. K., and A. P. Ker (1998): "Nonparametric Estimation of Crop Yield Distributions: Implications for Rating Group-Risk Crop Insurance Contracts," *American Journal Of Agricultural Economics*, 80(1), 139–153.

Goodwin, B. K., and A. K. Mishra (2006): "Are "Decoupled" Farm Program Payments Really Decoupled? An Empirical Evaluation," *American Journal of Agricultural Economics*, 88, 73–89.

Goodwin, B. K., A. K. Mishra, and F. Ortalo-Magné (2012): *The Intended and Unintended Effects of U.S. Agricultural and Biotechnology Policieschap*. The Buck Stops Where? The Distribution of Agricultural Subsidies. National Bureau of Economic Research, Edited by Joshua S. Graff Zivin and Jeffrey M. Perloff.

Goodwin, B. K., A. K. Mishra, and F. N. Ortalo-Magne (2003): "What's Wrong With our Models of Agricultural Land Values?," *American Journal Of Agricultural Economics*, 85(3), 744–752.

Goodwin, B. K., and N. E. Piggott (2020): "Has Technology Increased Agricultural Yield Risk? Evidence from the Crop Insurance Biotech Endorsement," *Amer. J. Agr. Econ.*, 102(5), 1578–1597.

Griliches, Z. (1957): "Hybrid Corn: An Exploration in the Economics of Technological Change," *Econometrica*, 25, 501–522.

_______ (1958): "Research Costs and Social Returns: Hybrid Corn and Related Innovations," *Journal of Political Economy*, 66, 419–431.

_______ (1964): "Research Expenditures, Education, and the Aggregate Agricultural Production Function," *American Economic Review*, 54, 961–974.

Guney, S., B. K. Goodwin, and A. Riquelme (2018): "Semi-Parametric Generalized Additive Vector Autoregressive Models of Spatial Basis Dynamics," *American Journal of Agricultural Economics*.

Hennessy, D. A. (1998): "The Production Effects of Agricultural Income Support Policies under Uncertainty," *American Journal of Agricultural Economics*, 80, 46–57.

Houck, J. P., and M. E. Ryan (1972): "Supply Analysis for Corn in the United States: The Impact of Changing Governmental Programs," *American Journal of Agricultural Economics*, 54, 184–191.

Hubbell, B. J., M. C. Marra, and G. A. Carlson (2000): "Estimating the Demand for a New Technology: Bt Cotton and Insecticide Policies," *American Journal of Agricultural Economics*, 82, 118–132.

Huffman, W. E., and M. D. Lange (1989): "Off-Farm Work Decisions of Husbands and Wives: Decision Making," *Review of Economics and Statistics*, 71, 471–80.

Jovanovic, B., and Y. Nyarko (1996): "Learning by Doing and the Choice of Technology," *Econometrica*, 64, 1299–1310.

Just, D. R., and R. E. Just (2016): "Empirical Identification of Behavioral Choice Models under Risk," *American Journal of Agricultural Economics*, 98(4), 1181–1194.

Just, D. R., and H. H. Peterson (2010): "Is Expected Utility Theory Applicable? A Revealed Preference Test," *American Journal of Agricultural Economics*, 92, 16–27.

Just, R., and R. Pope (1979): "Production Function Estimation and Related Risk Considerations," *American Journal of Agricultural Economics*, 61, 276–284.

_______ (2001): "The Agricultural Producer: Theory and Statistical Measurement," in *Handbook of Agricultural Economics*, ed. by B. Gardner, and G. Rausser. North Holland, Amsterdam.

Just, R. E., and R. D. Pope (1978): "Stochastic Specification of Production Functions and Economic Implications," *Journal of Econometrics*, 7(1), 67–86.

Just, R. E., D. Zilberman, and E. Hochman (1983): "Estimation of Multicrop Production Functions," *American Journal of Agricultural Economics*, 65, 770–780.

Just, R. E., D. Zilberman, E. Hochman, and Z. Bar-Shira (1990): "Input Allocation in Multicrop Systems," *American Journal of Agricultural Economics*, 72, 200–209.

Kalirajan, K. P., and R. T. Shand (1999): "Frontier Production Functions and Technical Efficiency Measures," *Journal of Economic surveys*, 13(2), 149–172.

Keith H. Coble, and J. W. G. Robert Dismukes (2007): "Private Crop Insurers and the Reinsurance Fund Allocation Decision," *American Journal of Agricultural Economics*, 89, 582–595.

Ker, A. P., and T. N. Tolhurst (2019): "On the Treatment of Heteroscedasticity in Crop Yield Data," *American Journal of Agricultural Economics*, 101(4), 1247–1261.

Kim, H. Y. (2005): "Aggregation Over Firms and Flexible Functional Forms," *The Economic Record*, 81(252), 19–29.

Kirwan, B. (2009): "The Incidence of U.S. Agricultural Subsidies on Farmland Rental Rates," *Journal of Political Economy*, 117, 138–164, Journal of Political Economy.

Kirwan, B. E., S. Uchida, and T. K. White (2012): "Aggregate and Farm-Level Productivity Growth in Tobacco: Before and After the Quota Buyout," *American Journal of Agricultural Economics*, 94, 838–853.

Kislev, Y., and W. Peterson (1981): "Induced Innovations and Farm Mechanization," *American Journal of Agricultural Economics*, 63, 562–65.

_______ (1982): "Prices, Technology and Farm Size," *Journal of Political Economy*, 90, 578–95.

Kuwayama, Y., A. Thompson, R. Bernknopf, B. Zaitchik, and P. Vail (2019): "Estimating the Impact of Drought on Agriculture using the U.S. Drought Monitor," *American Journal of Agricultural Economics*, 101(1), 193–210.

LaFrance, J. T., and R. D. Pope (2008): "Homogeneity and Supply," *American Journal Of Agricultural Economics*, 90, 606–612.

_______ (2010): "Duality Theory for Variable Costs in Joint Production," *American Journal of Agricultural Economics*, 92(3), 755–762.

Lichtenberg, E., and D. Zilberman (1986): "The Econometrics of Damage Control-Why Specification Matters," *American Journal of Agricultural Economics*, 68, 261–73.

Liu, Y., and C. R. Shumway (2008): "Induced Innovation in U.S. Agriculture: Timeseries, Direct Econometric, and Nonparametric Tests," *American Journal of Agricultural Economics*, (in press) Published Online: Jul 10 2008.

Lybbert, T. J., and D. R. Just (2007): "Is Risk Aversion Really Correlated with-Wealth? How Estimated Probabilities Introduce Spurious Correlation," *American Journal of Agricultural Economics*, 89, 964–979.

Mildenhall, S. J. (2006): "Correlation and Aggregate Loss Distributions with an Emphasis on the Iman-Conover Method," Casualty Actuarial Society Forum Casualty Actuarial Society — Arlington, Virginia, http://www.casact.org/pubs/forum/06wforum/06w107.pdf.

Mishra, A. K., and B. K. Goodwin (1997): "Farm Income Variability and the Supply of Off-Farm Labor," *American Journal Of Agricultural Economics*, 79(3), 880–887.

Morrison-Paul, C. (1997): "Structural Change, Capital Investment and Productivity in the Food Processing Industry," *American Journal of Agricultural Economics*, 79, 110–125.

Moschini, G. (2001): "Production Risk and the Estimation of Ex-Ante Cost Functions," *Journal of Econometrics*, 100, 357–80.

Moschini, G., and D. Hennessy (2001): "Uncertainty, Risk Aversion, and Risk Management for Agricultural Producers," in *Handbook of Agricultural Economics*, ed. by B. Gardner, and G. Rausser, vol. 1. North Holland, Amsterdam.

Moschini, G., and D. Moro (1994): "Autocorrelation Specification in Singular Equation Systems," *Economics Letters*, 46(4), 303–309.

Mundlak, Y. (1996): "Production Function Estimation: Reviving the Primal," *Econometrica*, 64, 431–438.

_______ (2001): "Production and supply," in *Handbook of Agricultural Economics*, ed. By B. Gardner, and G. Rausser, vol. 1. North Holland, Amsterdam.

O'Donnell, C. J. (2012): "Nonparametric Estimates of the Components of Productivity and Profitability Change in U.S. Agriculture," *American Journal of Agricultural Economics*, 94, 873–890.

Olmstead, A., and P. Rhode (1993): "Induced Innovation in American Agriculture: A Reconsideration," *Journal of Political Economy*, 101, 100–118.

Ozaki, V. A., S. K. Ghosh, B. K. Goodwin, and R. Shirota (2008): "Spatio-Temporal Modeling of Agricultural Yield Data with an Application to Pricing Crop Insurance Contracts," *American Journal Of Agricultural Economics*, (in press) Published Online: May 12 2008.

Plastina, A., and S. H. Lence (2019): "Theoretical Production Restrictions and Agricultural Technology in the United States," *American Journal of Agricultural Economics*, 101(3), 849–869.

Platoni, S., P. Sckokai, and D. Moro (2012): "Panel Data Estimation Techniques and Farm-level Data Models," *American Journal Of Agricultural Economics*, 94, 1202–1217.

Pope, R. (1982): "To Dual or Not to Dual," *Western Journal of Agricultural Economics*, 7, 337–351.

Pope, R. D., and R. E. Just (1996): "Empirical Implementation of Ex-Ante Cost Functions," *Journal of Econometrics*, 72, 231–249.

_______ (2002): "Random Profits and Duality," *American Journal of Agricultural Economics*, 84, 1–7.

_______ (2003): "Distinguishing Errors in Measurement from Errors in Optimization," *American Journal of Agricultural Economics*, 85, 348–58.

Roosen, J., and D. A. Hennessy (2003): "Tests for the Role of Risk Aversion on Input Use," *American Journal of Agricultural Economics*, 85(1), 30–43.

Rosas, F., and S. H. Lence (2019): "How Reliable is Duality Theory in EmpiricalWork?," *American Journal of Agricultural Economics*, 101(3), 825–848.

Rucker, R. R., W. N. Thurman, and D. A. Sumner (1995): "Restricting the Market for Quota: An Analysis of Tobacco Production Rights with Corroboration from Congressional Testimony," *Journal of Political Economy*, 103, 142–175.

Ryan, D. L., and T. J. Wales (1998): "A Simple Method for Imposing Local Curvature in Some Flexible Consumer-Demand Systems," *Journal of Business and Economic Statistics*, 16, 331–338.

Sandmo, A. (1971): "On the Theory of the Competitive Firm Under Price Uncertainty," *American Economic Review*, 61, 65–73.

Sumner, D. A. (1982): "The Off-Farm Labor Supply of Farmers," *American Journal of Agricultural Economics*, 64, 499–509.

Taylor, C. R. (1989): "Duality, Optimization, and Microeconomic Theory: Pitfalls for the Applied Researcher," *Western Journal of Agricultural Economics*, 14, 200–222.

Ubilava, D. (2018): "The Role of El Nino Southern Oscillation in Commodity Price Movement and Predictability," *American Journal of Agricultural Economics*, 100(1), 239–263.

Varian, H. R. (1984): "The Nonparametric Approach to Production Analysis," *Econometrica*, 52(3), 579–97.

Yan, J. (2006): "Enjoy the Joy of Copulas," Technical Report 365, Department of Statistics, University of Iowa, http://www.stat.uiowa.edu/techrep/tr365.pdf.

Zilberman, D., A. Schmitz, G. Casterline, E. Lichtenberg, and J. B. Siebert (1991): "The Economics of Pesticide Use and Regulation," *Science*, 253, 515–522.

Chapter 1

Production Theory

"Production" as a concept, generally begins with the "production function"

Production involves the process of transferring inputs (materials and forces) into outputs of goods or services

A production function in an engineering / technological concept devoid of economics

We often think in terms of "production plans" = quantities of each input + corresponding outputs

We may write as

$$\text{Netputs: } \{ -Z_1, -Z_2, \ldots, -Z_n, Z_{n+1} \}$$
$$\text{Inputs + Outputs: } \{x_1, \ldots, x_n, y\}$$

"Technology" = set of all production plans feasible for the current state of knowledge

We often define inputs as —

"Fixed" — cannot be altered during present production period
"Variable" — can be altered
"Long Run" — period long enough to allow all factors to be variable

Economists have no inherent interest in the production function as it is devoid of economic content — further, if it is possible to address produces behavior without directly considering the production function (i.e., through "Duality") — it is better

Production theory compared to utility theory —

— production/supply basics
  — can actually measure inputs/outputs
  — does not involve human behavior (at first glance)
  — output is a purely ordinal concept
— production/supply may be harder because you may need to consider
  — technological change
  — induced innovation

Production Function

$y(z) = 0$

z = net-valued of netputs (inputs + outputs) corresponding to a single period

Or — often written as —

$Y(y, x) = 0$ (separates inputs + outputs)

— Assume $y + x$ are non-negative
— Also — we are typically only concerned with inputs that are economically scarce and under control of decision makers (i.e. choice variables) — i.e., not things such as weather —
— such inputs are included in structures of $Y(.)$.
— For now, we will assume y is a scalar and solve $Y(.)$ for y —

$$y = f(x)$$

$f(.)$ = single valued function yielding max output for x

Formal properties of f(x):

1. a) Weak monotonicity: if $x' \geq x$, then $f(x') \geq f(x)$
   b) Strict monotonicity: if $x' > x$, then $f(x') \geq f(x)$

2. a) Quasic-concavity : $V(y) = \{X: f(x) \geq y\}$ is convex set
   b) Concavity: $f(\lambda x^0 + (1 - \lambda)x') \geq \lambda f(x^0) + (1 - \lambda) f(x')$
3. a) weak essentiality: $f(0, \ldots, 0) = 0$
   b) strict essentiality: $f(X, \ldots, 0, X_{k+1}, \ldots X_n) = 0$
4. V(y): set is closed + non-empty

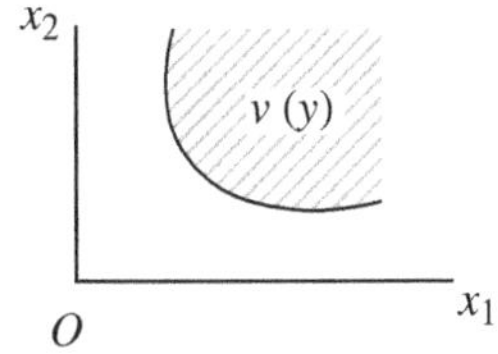

5. f(x) is finite, non-negative, single valued, real valued for all $X \in \mathbb{R}^+$
6. a) f(x) everywhere continuous
   b) f(x) twice differential
7. f(x) is homogeneous of degree θ : $f(k \cdot x) = k^\theta \cdot f(x)$
   $\Rightarrow$ First partial, homo. deg. θ-1 and, $\theta = 1 \Rightarrow$ homothetic production function (should be familiar)

   Euler's theorem holds: $= \sum f_i x_i = \theta f(x)$ where $f_i = \dfrac{\partial f}{\partial x_i}$

1a + 1b imply $f(x)$ monotonically increasing in inputs — rules out negative marginal products.

This excludes "Third Stage of Production" —

Recall Stage I: MP > AP >0
Stage II: AP > MP $\geq$ 0 * Relevant stage
Stage III: MP < 0

2a — Requires convex input set — implies diminishing MRTS
— or equivalently, if X^0 and X^1 can both be used to produce y, any weighted average can also

2b — Also implies, law of diminishing mp $\Rightarrow$ as any X is increased, associated marginal output must never increase
$\Rightarrow$ Hessian of $f(x)$ is negative semi-definite
— Also rules out Stage I

3b — Isoquant do not intersect axes

6a + b — made for mathematical convenience — no discrete jumps — allow us to use differential calculus

3 Important Examples —

1) Cobb-Douglas — $y = A \cdot \prod_i X_i^{\alpha i}$ $\quad \alpha_i > 0 \forall i$

$$mp_j = \frac{\partial f}{\partial x_j} = \alpha_j \frac{\prod_i X_i \alpha_i}{X_j} > 0 \; for \; \forall_i$$

(verifies monotonicity)

Does it verify concavity?

$$\frac{\partial^2 f}{\partial X_i} = \frac{\alpha_j(\alpha_j - 1)}{Xj^2} \prod_i X^{\alpha_i}$$

$\Rightarrow < 0$ only if $\alpha_j < 1$ so requires additional restriction to ensure concavity

Strong essentiality verified since any Xi = 0 ⇒ y = 0

2) Leontif – y = min $\{\alpha_1 X_1, \alpha_2 X_2, \ldots\}$
— Clearly satisfies monotonicity, but not strict monotonicity
— Verifies concavity

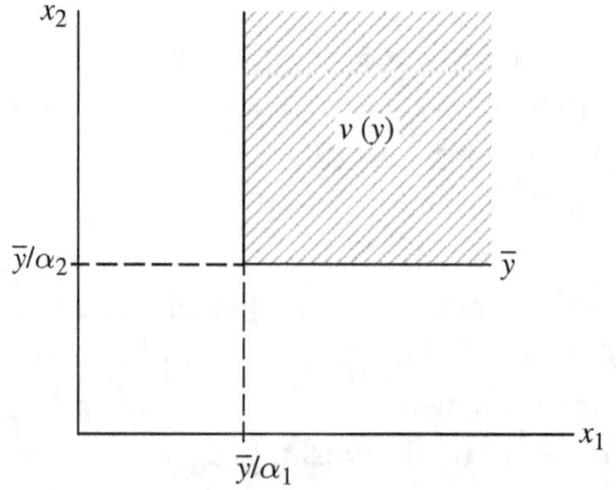

Consider production function $y = f(x_1, \bar{X}_2 = y / \alpha_2)$

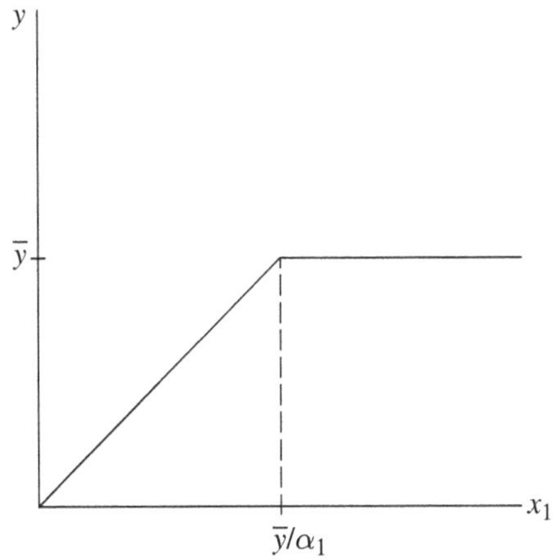

Note — law of diminishing marginal productivity is especially severe — mp = 0 for $X_1 > \bar{y}/\alpha_1$.

3. Constant Elasticity of substitution (Chambers also calls it Arrow, Chenery, Minhas, Solow (ACMS) function)

$$f(x) = \beta\left[a_1 X^{(\sigma-1)/\sigma} + a_2 X_2^{(\sigma-1)\sigma}\right]^{\frac{\sigma}{\sigma-1}}$$

σ = Elasticity of substitution (see below).

Characterizing Production Functions

Several concepts —

1) Elasticity of $\underset{\text{(input)}}{\text{Output}}$ $= \epsilon_i = \dfrac{\partial f}{\partial X_i} \cdot \dfrac{X_i}{y} = \dfrac{MPi}{AP_i}$

2) Law of variables propertions — Also known as law of diminishing return — if we hold $\forall\ X_i\ i \neq j$ constant and increase X_j – MP_j must eventually fall.

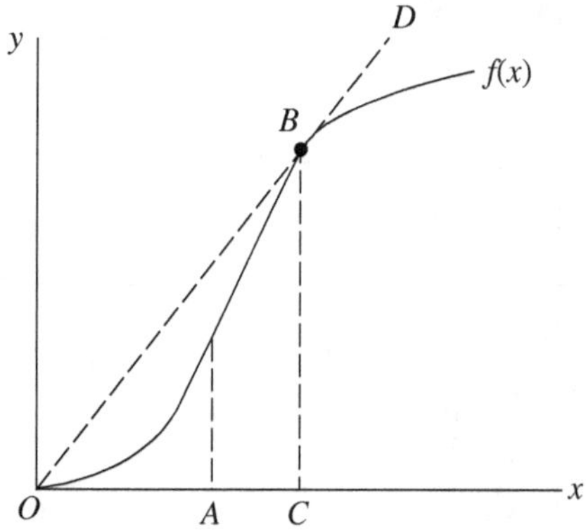

A = inflection point = point of max MP falls after
AP is maximized where AP = MP — given by tangency

For X < C ⇒ Stage I
For X > C but Mp > 0 (always as we have drawn it) ⇒ Stage II
Point B often called the "extensive margin" of production

3) Elasticity of Scale —
$$E = \left.\frac{\partial \ln f(\lambda x)}{\partial \ln \lambda}\right/_{\lambda=1}$$ = Measure of output change for a specific increase in input bundle

If $\in = 1 \Rightarrow$ CRS
$\in < 1 \Rightarrow$ DRS
$\in > 1 \Rightarrow$ IRS

Relationship between elasticity of scale and elasticities of outputs —

$$\left.\frac{\partial \ln f(\lambda x)}{\partial \ln \lambda}\right|_{\lambda=1} = \sum_i \frac{\partial f}{\partial X_i} \cdot \frac{X_i}{y} = \sum_i \in_i$$

Measures of Input Substitutability

One of the most significant debates of ag econ, involves the degree of substitutability, among inputs.

— often, researchers assume $\sigma = 0$ (Leontief Technologies) for convenience

— Argue if is impossible to substitute for some inputs — such as basic farm output

We will assume that strict monotonicity, concavity, and continuity (trial differentiability) holds.

Define $\overline{V}(y)$ = lower boundary of $V(y)$

$\overline{V}(y) = \{x : f(x) = y\}$

Solve $y = f(x)$ for a single X_i (in terms of other X_j and y) —

$$X_i^* = X_i\,(X_1,\ \dots\ ,X_{i-1},\ \dots,\ X_n)$$

Substitute this into $y = f(x)$ for X_i

$$y = f(x_1,\ \dots,\ X_i^*,\ \dots\ X_n)$$

Differentiate w.r.t. X_j

$$\frac{\partial f}{\partial x_i}\cdot\frac{\partial X_i}{\partial X_j}+\frac{\partial f}{\partial X_j}=0$$

Solve for $\dfrac{\partial X_i}{\partial X_j} = -\dfrac{\partial f/\partial X_j}{\partial f/\partial X_i} = MRTS$

= Adjustment in X_i needed to maintain $\overline{V}(y)$ when X_j is changed.

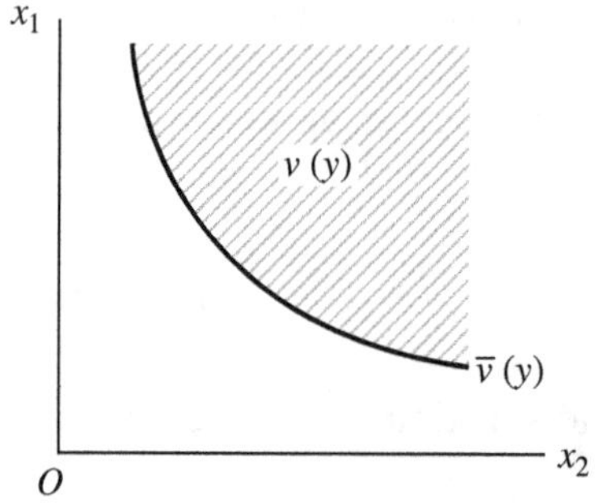

MRTS = slope if $\bar{v}(y)$

Many different measures of degree of substitutability among inputs

Hicks Elasticity of Substitution

$$\sigma_{ij} = \frac{\partial(X_j/X_i)}{\partial(f_i/f_j)} \cdot \frac{f_i/f_j}{X_j/X_i} = \frac{\partial \ln(X_i/X_j)}{\partial \ln(f_i/f_j)}$$

For Leontief, $\sigma = 0$
For linear isoquant, $\sigma = \infty$
For 2 inputs, $\sigma \geq 0$ always (due to convex $v(y)$)

Measures of substitutability not as meaningful in case of 2 inputs — since we always have $\sigma \geq 0$.

Consider case of 3 inputs — $y = f(X_1, X_2, X_3)$

Now, we used to think of isoquant for i, j — holding k constant.

Cofactor – $A_{n \times n}$

A_{ij} = A with row i, col j deleted

Cofactor $ij = (-1)^{i+j}.\det(A_{ij})$

Transpose of cofactor ij = Adjoint at A

3 possible isoquants – $X_1 - X_2$, holding 3 constant
$X_2 - X_3$ ' 1 '
$X_1 - X_3$ " 2 "

In this case, there are 3 standard measures of input substitutability —

1) Direct elasticity of substitution —
   — A simple generalisation of the Hick's eos —

$$\sigma_{ij}^{D} = \left(\frac{\partial(X_i / X_j)}{\partial(f_i / f_j)} \cdot \frac{f_i / f_j}{X_j / X_i} \right) \Bigg|_{X_k = \bar{X}_k} \quad \forall k \neq i, j$$

Represents a short-run elasticity gives of offeres all other inputs are held constant

Define H = for bordered Hession of prod. function

F_{ij} = cofactor associated with f_{ij}

F = determinant of H

This lead us to a second measure of input substitution —

Also

Allen-Uzawa by Cost function

$$= \sigma_{ij} = \frac{C(\cdot) \cdot C_{ij}}{C_i \cdot C_j}$$

2) Allen partial elasticity of substitution —

$$\sigma_{ij} = \sum_i \frac{X_i f_i}{X_i X_j} \cdot \frac{F_{ji}}{F}$$

Note, in 2 input case: $\sigma_{ij}^{D} \equiv \sigma_{ij}$

Note — both are symmetric (by Young's Theorem)

$\sigma_{ij} < 0 \Rightarrow$ complements

$\sigma_{ij} > 0 \Rightarrow$ substitutes

3) Morishima Elasticity of Substitutions

Argued to be a better measure of substitution relationships (see Blackorby + Russell) (exact measures of how X_i/X_j changes as w_i/w_j changes)

$$\sigma_{ij}^{M} = \frac{f_i}{X_i} \cdot \frac{F_{ji}}{F} - \frac{f_i}{X_i} \cdot \frac{F_{ij}}{F}$$

Note that there is a direct relationship between σ_{ij} and σ_{ij}^{m}

$$\sigma_{ij}^{m} = \frac{f_i}{f_i} \cdot \frac{X_i}{X_i} (\sigma_{ij} - \sigma_{jj})$$

This illustrates several important points —

— σ_{ij}^{m} and σ_{ij} can be of opposite signs
— e.g., if $|\sigma_{ij}| < |\sigma_{ji}| \Rightarrow \sigma_{ij}^{m} > 0$ even
if $\sigma_{ij} < 0$
— if $\sigma_{ij} > 0$ then $\sigma_{ij}^{m} > 0$ always
— symmetry does not hold for σ_{ij}^{m} —

so i and j could be substitutes that j and i complements
suppose $|\sigma_{ii}| > |\sigma_{ji}| > |\sigma_{ij}|$, then —

$\sigma_{ij}^{m} < 0$ (Moroshima complements)
$\sigma_{ji}^{m} > 0$ (Moroshima substitutes)

The Morishima *EOS* is preferred as an "economic" measure of substitutability — we will discuss this is greater detail later.

Separability in Production Functions

In order to simplify and make problems tractable — we want to break production into separable stages.

e. g. — Auto production

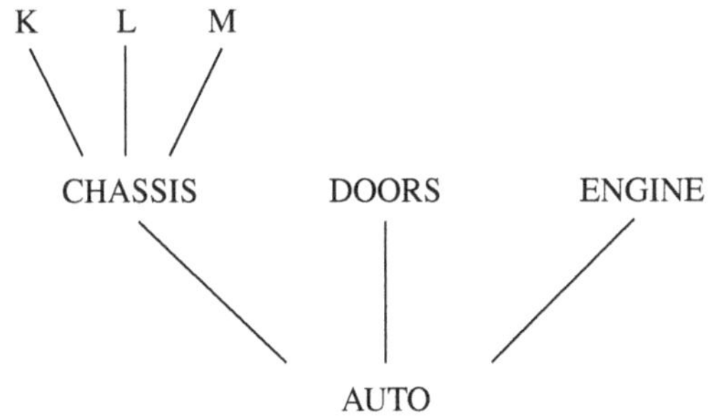

Can we trust treat stages independently?
Separability is a question of low $MRTS_{ij}$ responds to ΔX_k
We say X_i and X_j are separable from X_k if

$$\frac{\partial\left(\dfrac{\partial f / \partial x_i}{\partial f / \partial x_j}\right)}{\partial x_k} = 0 \Rightarrow \quad \text{Slope of isozuant in } i-j \text{ space not affected by } dX_k$$

This implies $\frac{\partial \ln f_i}{\partial \ln x_k} = \frac{\partial \ln f_j}{\partial \ln X_k}$

There are several versions of separability, depending on grouping of i, j, k (note — fully analogous to separability in demand) —

1) Weak separability —

$$\frac{\partial\left(\dfrac{\partial f / \partial x_i}{\partial f / \partial x_j}\right)}{\partial x_k} = 0 \qquad i, j \in \mathrm{I}, k \notin I$$

I = subgroup of inputs

This implies we can write overall production function in terms of "sub-functions"

$$f(x) = F(f_1(X^1), f_2(X^2)\ldots.)$$

Implies "production trees" — "multi-stage production"

2) Strong separability —

$$\frac{\partial\left(\dfrac{\partial f/\partial x_i}{\partial f/\partial x_j}\right)}{\partial x_k}=0 \qquad i\in I,\ j\in G,\ k\in H$$

$$H\neq G, I$$

Also called additive separability — can write overall production function as —

$$f(x)=F(f_1(X^1)+f_2(x^2)+\ldots+f_n(x^n))$$

3) Factor-wise separability — if each partition I,G,H contain a single input

$$\frac{\partial\left(\dfrac{\partial f/\partial x_i}{\partial f/\partial x_j}\right)}{\partial x_k}=0 \qquad \forall i\neq j\neq k$$

$$f(x)=F(X_1+X_2+\ldots)$$

This allows for nonessential inputs (violates one of our assumptions)

Separability suggests parametric restructions on production (and cost/profit) functions which can be imposed/tested.

Empirical Estimation of Production Functions

(Mundlak 2001 Handbook Chapter) — points worth noting/repeating —

1) Economists generally not interested in this — it is a purely technical relationship
2) We often refer to this as the "primal" problem.
3) Much empirical work on this topic — began by Cobb-Douglas (1928) — and greatly elaborated by (Heads) in 1940s–1970s. Cobb-Douglas cornerstone of empirical work
4) Empirical estimates are not robust

5) Empirical estimates often show significant gap between VMP + W (factor prices)
6) Big problems associated with addressing differences in input quantity — e.g., how do we measures quantity of K+L? How do we distinguish stocks+flows? (e.g., K)
7) Inputs are endogenous — OLS biased and inconsistent.

Muullak (1996, 2001) provides a detailed discussion of empirical issues relating to the estimation of production functions.

Muullak has written extensively on the empirical situation on this topic.

Consider the problem of estimating a production function using panel data

Single input case

$$Y = AX^{B} e^{m_0 + u_0}$$

mo = firm specific fixed effect (known to the firm, but not to econometrican)

Uo = random shock not known when decisions are made.

Expected output , given input, for firm i is —

(1) $Y_i^e = E(Y / x_i) \approx AX_i^{B} e^{moi}$

Note we ignore $E(e^{u_0}) = (1 + \sigma_u^2 / 2)$ where $\sigma_u^2 = E(u_o)$

Assume P is known and that firm chooses X to max Π —

$$\max_{x_i} \prod^e (Xw; p) = pY_i^e - wX_i$$

FOC's

(2) $\beta AX^{\beta - 1} = \frac{W}{p} e^{m_1 + u_i}$

Where m_1 = deviation known to firm but not econometrician this is a firm-specific effect, invariant over time, generally not equal to zero, it might represent factor specific to a firm's expectation function or utility function parameters

u_1 = errors that firm makes in optimization — transitory and averages zero

we can separate all variables in the terms as differences from overall sample mean —

$$z_{it}\ \ln(z_{it}) - \left(\sum_i \sum_t \ln(z_{it})/n\right)$$

$n = \mathrm{N} \cdot \mathrm{T}$, N = # firm
T = # time periods
Rewrite (1) + (2) —

$$y_{it} - X_{it}\beta = m_{oi} + u_{oit}$$
$$y_{it} - x_{it} = w_{it} + m_{1t} + u_{1it} + u_{oit}$$

solve for reduced from for x_{it} —

$$x_{it} = -\ c(p_{it} + u_{1it} + m_{\mathrm{it}} - m_{oi})\ \text{where c} = (\mathrm{r}\beta)^{-1}$$

so 4 error components —
u_o = unknown production shock ~ $(0, \sigma_{00})$
u_1 = optimization error ~ $(0, \sigma_{11})$
m_0 = firm specific production effect ~ (m_0, τ_{00})
m_1 = firm specific expectation/utility effect ~ (m_1, τ_{11})
expected cross products, all zero (unconditional)
Point#1 — since optional input choice x_{it} is a function of firm effect m_{ot} — input is clearly endogenous ⇒ bias of OLS + lack of robustness
How to overcome endogeneity?
Another possibility for estimation — the "Dual Estimate" (uses price as an instrumental variable) —

$$\hat{\delta}_p = p'y/p'x \rightarrow$$

$$y = x\gamma + m_0 + u_0$$
$$p'y = p'x\gamma + p'(m_0 + u_0)$$

solve for $\gamma \rightarrow$

$$\frac{p'y}{p'x} = \gamma + \frac{p'}{p'x}(m_0 + u_0)$$

Take expectations —

$$E\left(\frac{p'y}{p'x}\right) = \gamma + E\left(\frac{p'm_0}{p'x} + \frac{p'u_0}{p'x}\right)$$

Since p is uncorrelated with m_0 and u_0 — and since $E(m_0) = E(u_0) = 0$

$$E\left(\frac{p'y}{p'x}\right) = \gamma \Rightarrow unbiased$$

However — note that information about optimization error u, never surfaces in this estimate —

Thus — dual estimates is not fully efficient as some information about structures of problem is being ignored, Also — depends on assumption that p is exogenous — if data are at market level rather than firm level — this is not a valid assumption. Also — p may be fixed cross-sectionally if markets are integrated — Another possibility — a Fixed Effects (within) estimates — (work with deviations from cross-sectional means) —

Called "within estimates" because it depends on within firm variation.

The differencing removes the factor that is causing the problem — i.e, m_0 — which is firm specific and invariant over time

$$x_{it} - \bar{x}_i = -c(p_{it} - p_i + u_{lit} - u_{li})$$

$\Rightarrow$firm effect disappeared — estimates are unbiased.

Mundlak (1996, 2001) also discusses other possibilities, including a "hybrid" IV estimator

In 2001 Handbook paper, Mundlak reviews empirical work for agriculture — some key findings —

1) Elasticity of labor never exceeds 0.5 — typically in range 0.25 – 0.45 — far below findings for non-ag industries
2) Implies agriculture is capital-intensive
3) Labor elasticity seems to have declined over time — indicating technical change has been labor saving.
4) In country studies — elasticity of land has been between 0 – 1/3
5) Sum of labor and land elasticites in ag. ≈ 0.50 — relevant to solve of farm income going to labor and land.
6) $\Sigma\varepsilon_i$ = Measure of scale elasticity — typically > 1 leading some authors to conclude that ag — has IRS — Mundlak says more likely this neglects biases that he noted (e.g. endogenous X)
7) Many differences across studies ⇒ lack of robustness Mundlak argues this has stimulated research in 3 directions —
   - — overcoming simultaneity from endogenous inputs
   - — Algebraic form of production function
   - — Allow for endogenous technology

The Dual Approach — Cost + Profit Functions

What do use mean by "duality"

Basic idea in that it makes no difference if one uses the production function to develop explicit cost minimizing factor demands (the primal approach) — or one starts from the optimized cost function and derives the factor demands (via Hotelling's Lemma — the dual approach).

Pope discusses the conceptual background — which came from the linear programming literature

Minkowski's Theorem — every closed convex set $v(y) = \{X: f(x) \geq y\}$ t can be characterized by its supporting half-space —

A half space (convex curve) is a surface of a vector space V – $H(x) = \{x: Z(x) \geq y\}$

So — two obvious examples —

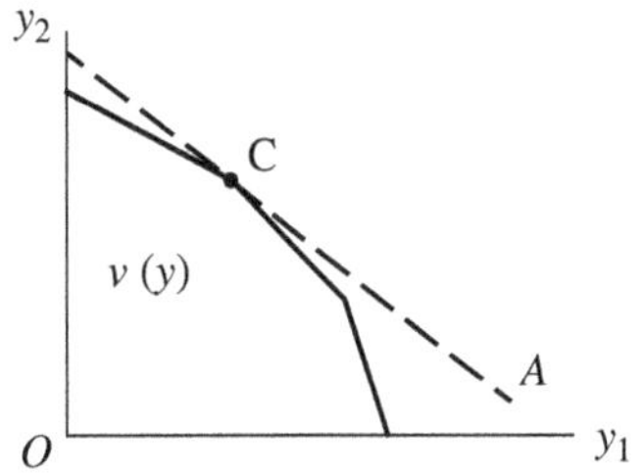

Outputs y_1 , y_2 – could be fully described by set of isoprofit lines like A

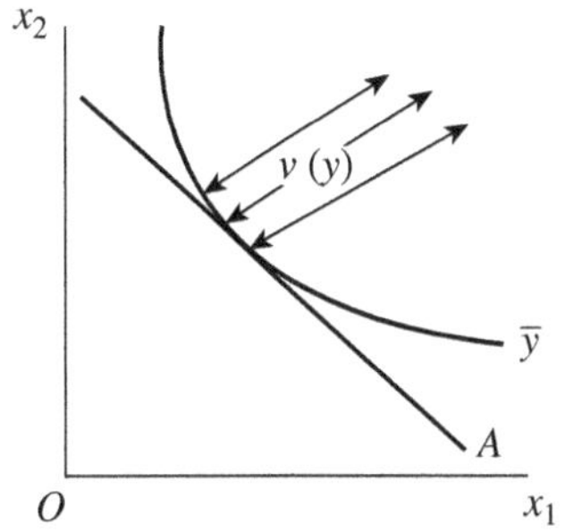

Isoquant for $\bar{y}$ could be fully described by altering iso-cost lines A
⇒ cost function is dual to isoquants

Gorman characterized duality as simply referring to the choice of independent variables one uses to describe/ define a theory.

In production — some technology contains the optimal choice of inputs — observing these optimal inputs will allow us to describe technology.

In here, we will approach the dual problem through the cost, profit, and distance functions.

The Cost Functions

$$C(w,y) = \min_{x \geq 0} \{\text{w.x: x} \in v(y)\}$$

we assume, $\forall\ x > 0$, prices are exogenous.

Properties of the cost function —

1) $c(w,y) > 0$ for $w > 0$, $y > 0$ (non-negativity)
2) If $w' \geq w$ then $c(w',y) \geq c(w,y)$ (non decreasing in w)
3) $c(w,y)$ is concave and continuous in w

4) $c(t{\cdot}w,y) = t{\cdot}c(w,y)$ — linear homogeneity (homothetic in w)
5) If $y' \geq y$, $c(w,y') \geq c(w,y)$ (non-decreasing y)
6) $c(w, 0) = 0$ (no fixed costs)

These are all familiar to you and we will not bother with an extensive review — but a few comments are useful —

1) linear homogeneity — if you double all input prices, production costs exactly double. Also implies doubling all prices do not affect cost minimizing choice of inputs.
2) No fixed costs⇒ analogous to weak essentiality analogous to assuming we are dealing with long-term
   Shephard's Lemma —

$$\frac{\partial c(w,y)}{\partial w_i} = x_i(w,y) = i^{th}\text{cost-minimizing factor demand}$$

Note — we often work with logarithmic cost functions —

$$\frac{\partial \ln c(w,y)}{\partial \ln w_i} = \frac{\partial c(.)/c(.)}{\partial w_i / w_i} = \frac{x_i \cdot w_i}{c()} = \text{cost share}_i$$

Intuition of Shephard's Lemma

Consider relationship of cost function and low cost would change if w_j is altered, holding all inputs fixed

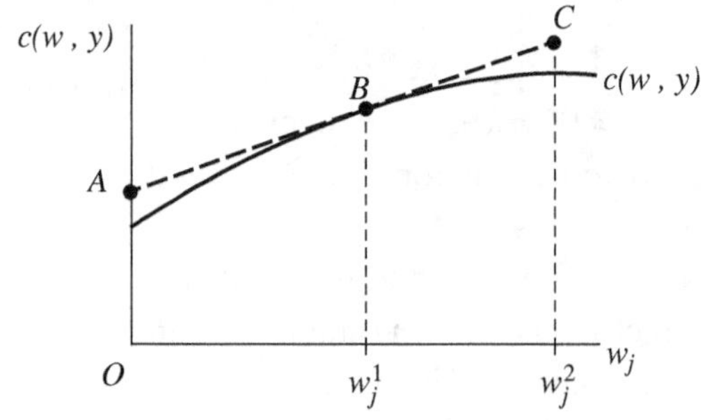

$C(w, y)$ = cost function

ABC = cost as Δw_j, holding $x_{it} - \bar{x}_i \forall_i$

B = cost of cost minimizing input bundle at w_j'.

By concavity, given B is point on cost function, entire function must lie beneath ABC.

Slope $c(w, y)$ = slope ABC at w_j'

But — derivative of ABC w.r.t. w_j' is X_j' at point B —

$$\text{thus} \quad \frac{\partial \text{ABC}}{\partial w_d} = \left.\frac{\partial c(f, y)}{\partial w_j}\right|_{w_j'} = x_j$$

* Comparative status of w_j changes —

By Shephard's Lemma —

$$\frac{\partial^2 c(p, y)}{\partial w_j^2} = \frac{\partial x_j}{\partial w_j}$$

$c(p,y)$ is homo. deg. 1 $\Rightarrow X_j$ homo deg 0

* concavity of $c(p,y)$

Define J = Hessian of c

— J is negative semi-definite + symmetric

— all own factor demand elasticity are $\in_{li} \leq 0$

— By Young's theorem — $\frac{\partial x_i}{\partial w_j} = \frac{\partial x_j}{\partial w_i}$

* Derived Demand Elasticity —

$$\in_{ij} \equiv \frac{\partial X_i(w, y)}{\partial w_0} \cdot \frac{w_j}{X_i} = \frac{\partial^2 c(w, y)}{\partial w_i \, \partial w_j} \cdot \frac{\omega_j}{x_i}$$

$$\in_{ii} \leq 0$$

Homogeneity implies $\Sigma_j \in_{ij} = 0$

Define $S_k = w_k \cdot x_k / c(p,y)$ = cost share k

We know — $S_i \in_{ij} = S_j \in_{ji}$
So, only if $S_i = S_j$ does $\in_{ij} = \in_{ji}$
* Homogeneity of cost function implies —

$$\frac{\partial c(t \cdot w, y)}{\partial y} = t \cdot \frac{\partial c(w, y)}{\partial y}$$

$\Rightarrow$ MC is linearly homogeneous in input prices
*Note — all inputs are identical to case for utility — compensated (Hicksian) demand functions in consumer case.
* cost function for Leontief case —

$$c(w, y) = y \cdot \sum \frac{w_i}{\alpha_i}$$

Which yields factor demands —
$x_i = \frac{y}{\alpha_i} \Rightarrow$ independent of prices
(This makes perfect sense intuitively)
* Cost Flexibility and Economics of Size and Scale —
Consider scale effect on input demand —

$$\frac{\partial x_i}{\partial y} = \frac{\partial^2 c(p,y)}{\partial w_i \partial y} = \begin{matrix}\text{By young's} \\ \text{theorem}\end{matrix} = \frac{\partial \left(\partial c(p,y) \middle/ \partial y \right)}{\partial w_i}$$

$$= \partial \text{mc} / \partial w_i \qquad \begin{matrix} < 0 \Rightarrow \text{“Inferior” input} \\ > 0 \Rightarrow \text{“Normal” input} \end{matrix}$$

Of course, since $\partial c / \partial y \geq 0$ (by assumption), we know that not all $\partial x_i / \partial y$ can be negative
* Homogeneity also implies —

$$\sum_i w_i \cdot \frac{\partial x_i}{\partial y} = \sum_i w_i \frac{\partial^2 c}{\partial y\, \partial w_i} = \frac{\partial c(w, y)}{\partial y}$$

* cost flexibility = MC/AC →

$$cta_n(w, y) = \frac{\partial c}{\partial y} \cdot \frac{y}{c} = \mathrm{MC}/_{\mathrm{AC}} = \frac{\partial \ln c}{\partial \ln y}$$

$$= \text{Elasticity of costs wrt output}$$

Reciprocal of $n = n^{-1}$ = Elast of size

If $n > 1 \Rightarrow$ diseconomies of size
$n = 1 \Rightarrow$ constant returns to size
$n < 1 \Rightarrow$ economics of size

Note n(w,y) is reciprocal value of the elasticity of scale $\in$ (x,y) at the cost-min combination of inputs

(see Chambers for a proof)

Intuitively —

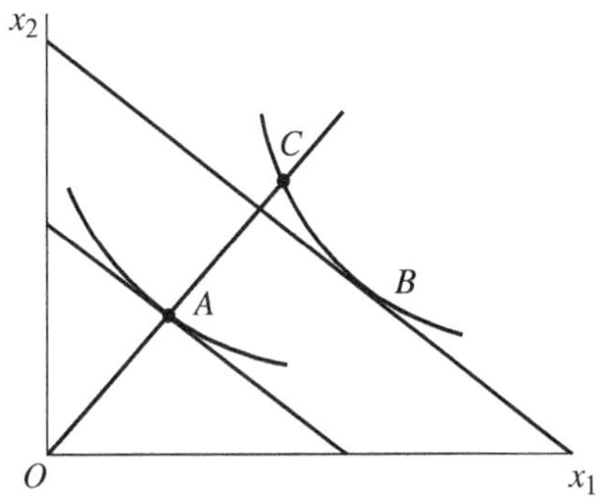

A-B represents how costs change as output changes, holding prices fixed

A-B is measured by elasticity of size

A-C is measure of output percentage change moving along a ray

2 Points —

1) If the ray is drawn through B — representing the points of tangency (i.e cost min/optimal production) — the points are identical. So, only at optimum is $n^{-1} = \in$.
2) An exception — homothetic technologies — in which case, they are equivalent always.

Measuring Elasticities of Substitution Using Cost Functions

Recall two points —

1) $\sigma \equiv \frac{d \ln(x_2/x_1)}{d \ln(f_1/f_2)}$
2) cost minimization requires $\text{MRTS}_{ij} = w_i/w_j$
   Which implies — $\sigma = \frac{d \ln(x_2/x_1)}{d \ln(w_1/w_2)}$
   So — σ can be interpreted as elasticity of an input ratio w.r.t prices

ratio

Another way to write it, using $\hat{X}_j = {}^{dx_j}\!/_{x_j}$

$$\sigma = \frac{\hat{x}_2 - \hat{x}_1}{\hat{w}_1 - \hat{w}_2}$$

Because w_i and x_i are readily available in the cost function, cost function can be used to derive input substitution elasticties (i.e. — do not have to go to prod./function)

⇒ A duality result.

Consider the cost-min problem —

Min $w' \cdot x$ s. t. $f(x) = y$

$L = w' \cdot x + \lambda (y - f(x))$

FOC's – $w_i - \lambda\, \partial f / \partial x_i = 0$ (n of these)

$y - f(x) = 0$ (1 of these)

Now, totally differentiate them
define $\forall_x f(x)$ = gradient = $[\partial f/\partial x_1 \ldots \partial f/\partial x_1]$
Total differentiation yields —

$$\lambda \begin{bmatrix} 0 & \forall_x f(x) \\ \forall_x f(x) & \forall_{xx} f(x) \end{bmatrix} \begin{bmatrix} \hat{\lambda} \\ dx \end{bmatrix} = \begin{bmatrix} dy \\ dw \end{bmatrix}$$

gradient Hessian

Define B = inverse of gradient and Hessian and solve —

$$\begin{bmatrix} \hat{\lambda} \\ dx \end{bmatrix} = \lambda^{-1} \mathrm{B} \begin{bmatrix} dy \\ dw \end{bmatrix}$$

Note B_{ij} is nxn with elements b_{ij} —

$$\text{This implies — } \frac{\partial x_i(w, y)}{\partial w_j} = \frac{b_{ij}}{\lambda}$$

Which, if we solve for the inverse, yielding B, is —

$$\frac{\partial x_i(w, y)}{\partial w_i} = \frac{F_{ji}}{F\lambda}$$

Where F_{ji} = cofactor element of Bordered Hessian of prod function
F = determinant of Bordered Hessian
Now, overall definition of Allen elasticity of sub —

$$\sigma_{ij} = \frac{F_{ji}}{F} \cdot \sum_i \left(\frac{\partial f}{\partial x_i} \right) x_i \bigg/ x_i x_j$$

$$\text{And note — } \in_{ij} = \frac{\partial x_i}{\partial w_j} \cdot \frac{w_j}{x_i} = \frac{F_{ji}}{F\lambda} \cdot \frac{w_j}{x_i}$$

Together, these implies —

$$\sigma_{ij} = \frac{c(w, y)}{w_j x_j} \cdot \in_{ij} = \frac{\in_{ij}}{S_i}$$

$$\frac{1}{s_j} = \text{inverse of cost share}$$

So – $\sigma_{ij} = \in_{ij}/S_j$ =Direct relationship between eos and price elasticity
An implication ⇒ σ_{ij} and $\in_{ij}$ contain the same information
Now, recall from Morishima elasticities —

$$\sigma_{ij}^{m} = \frac{f_j}{f_i} \cdot \frac{x_j}{x_i} (\sigma_{ij} - \sigma_{jj})$$

which, with a small degree of arranging, yields —

$$\sigma_{ij}^{m} = \in_{ij} - \in_{jj}$$

Again — note the implication that, if inputs are Allen substitutes, they must be Morishima substitutes (since $\in_{ji} < 0$ by concavity) but not vice versa.

A final concept, note that, by Shephard's Lemma —

$$\hat{C} = \frac{dc}{c} = S_i \hat{w}_i + S_j \hat{w}_j$$

which yields concept of a "Shadow Elast of Sub" — reflecting movements along a given factor price function at constant costs —

$$\sigma_{ij}^{s} = \frac{S_i}{S_i + S_j} \cdot \sigma_{ij}^{m} + \frac{S_j}{S_i + S_j} \sigma_{ij}^{m}$$

σ_{ij}^{s} is symmetric (a weighted average of σ^{m} terms)

Fixed Inputs and Short-Term Costs

Assume some inputs are fixed in short-term (x^2) and partition input set according: $x = (x^1, x^2)$

Some results for short-term cost function $c(w^1, y.x^2)$ —

1) $c(w^1, y, x^2)$ still satisfies Shephard's Lemma in w^1
2) $c(w^1, y, x^2)$ is non increasing in x^2 —

$$x^2 \geq x^{2}* \Rightarrow c(w^1, y, x^2) \leq c(w^1, y, x^{2*})$$

This is simple application of *Le* Chatelier principle —

Define S.R cost function —

$$c^s(w, y, x^2) = c(w^1, y, x^{2*}) + w^2x^2$$

if decision makers are rational —

$$c(w, y) = \min_{x^2} c(w^1, y, x^{2*}) + w^2x^2$$

And —

$$c(w, y) \leq c^s(w^1, y, x^2) \text{ and } c(w, y) = c^s(w^1, y, x^2(w, y))$$

graphical view —

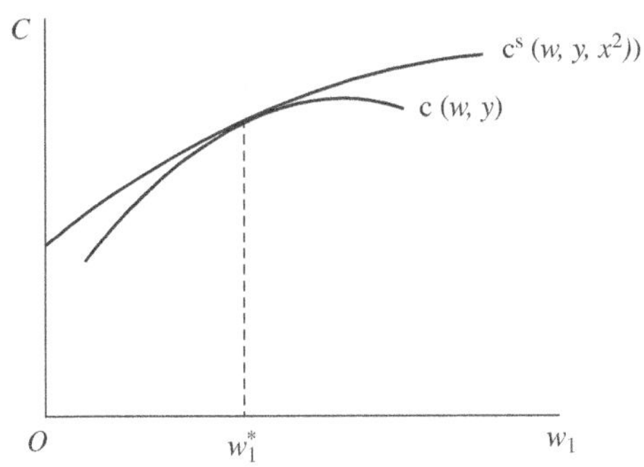

$c(w,y)$ = lower envelope for all $c^s c(.)$

Note — $c(w,y)$ is "more concave" than $c^s(.)$

$$\text{At } w_1^* - \frac{\partial c(w,y)}{\partial w_i} = \frac{\partial c^s(w,y,x^2)}{\partial w.}$$

$$\Rightarrow x_i(w, y) = x_i\,(w, y, x^2(w, y))$$

where x^2 here is bundle that minimizes by long run costs (i.e., bundle to w_1)
Greater concavity of long term costs implies —

$$\frac{\partial x_i(w,y)}{\partial w_i} \leq \frac{\partial x_i(w,y,x^2(w,y))}{\partial w_i} \quad \{\text{see Chambers for proof}$$

Separability of Cost Functions

We say, w_i and w_j are separable from w_k if —

$$\frac{\partial\left(\dfrac{\partial c/\partial w_j}{\partial w_k}\right)}{\partial w_k} = 0$$

Note, by Shephard's Lemma, this implies —
$i + j$ are separable of $\in_{ik} = \in_{jk}$, or —

$$\frac{\partial x_i(w,y)/\partial w_k}{x_i} = \frac{\partial x_j(w,y)/\partial w_k}{x_j}$$

1) Weak separability of cost function —

$$\frac{\partial\left(\dfrac{\partial c/\partial w_j}{\partial c/\partial w_k}\right)}{\partial w_k} = 0 \qquad \text{for } i, j \in I, \quad k \in G, \quad I \neq G$$

Which implies separable cost function of the form — $c(y, c^1(y, w^1), c^2(y, w^2)\ldots.)$

(Recall analogous result for production functions)

2) Strong separability of $c(w,y)$ —

$$\frac{\partial\left(\dfrac{\partial c/\partial w_i}{\partial c/\partial w_j}\right)}{\partial w_k}=0 \qquad i\in I,\quad j\in J,\quad k\notin IUJ$$

Which yields additively separable cost function —

$$c(w,y)=c\left(f(y),\left(\sum_i C^i(w^i,y)^{p(y)}\right)^{1/p(y)}\right)$$

3) Price wise separability — each group contains a single factor (as before).

Relationship between separability of cost and production functions —

$c(w,y)$ is dual to $f(x)$ BUT separability in $f(x)$ does not necessarily mean separability in $c(w,y)$.

An exception occurs for homothetic "sub-production" function —

If $f(x)$ is weakly separable and $f^i(x_I)$ of $y=f(f^1(x^1),f^2(x^2),\ldots)$ is homothetic then (w,y) is also weakly separable.

The Profit Function

Not a great deal of difference from cost function.

Definition: $\Pi(p,w)=\max_{x\geq 0}\{pf(x)-wx\}$

which is equivalent to: $\max_{x\geq 0}\{py-c(w,y)\}$

properties of $\Pi(p,w)$

1) $\Pi(p,w) \geq 0$
2) For $p^1 \geq p^2$, $\Pi(p^1, w) \geq \Pi(p^2, w)$ {non decreasing in p}
3) For $w^1 \geq w^2$, $\Pi(p, w^1) \leq \Pi(p, w^2)$ {non increasing in w}
4) $\Pi(p, w)$ is convex and continuous in (p, w)
5) $\Pi(t \cdot p, w) = t\,\Pi(p, w)$ {linear homogeneity}

Hotelling's lemma —

$$\frac{\partial \Pi(p,w)}{\partial p} = y(p,w) = \text{profit max supply}$$

And — $\dfrac{\partial \Pi(p,w)}{\partial w} = x(p,w)$ profit — max derived demand

Symmetry conditions —

Consider Hessian matrix of form —

$$\begin{bmatrix} \partial^2 \Pi \big/ \partial p^2 & \partial^2 \Pi \big/ \partial p \partial w^1 \\ \partial^2 \Pi \big/ \partial w \partial p & \partial^2 \Pi \big/ \partial w^2 \end{bmatrix}$$

Will be — symmetric

— positive semi-definite.

(Result of convexity of $\Pi(p,w)$)

Note importance of continuity to arrive at these results.

Implications of Hotelling's Lemma /symmetry —

$$\frac{\partial y(p,w)}{\partial p} \geq 0 \qquad \frac{\partial x_i(p,w)}{\partial w_i} \leq 0$$

$$\frac{\partial x_i}{\partial w_j} = \frac{\partial x_j}{\partial w_i} \text{ and } \frac{\partial y(p,w)}{\partial w_i} = -\frac{\partial x_i(p,w)}{\partial p}$$

Another implication of Hotellings Lemma is to substitute $y(p, w)=y^*$ into $x(w, y) \rightarrow$

(Note this uses result that cost-min and profit max are identical solutions) —

$$x(p, w) = x(w, y^{+}(p,w))$$

Differentiation Yields

$$\frac{\partial x_i(p,w)}{\partial p} = \frac{\partial x(w,y^*)}{\partial y} \cdot \frac{\partial y(p,w)}{\partial p}$$

And —

$$\frac{\partial x_i(p,w)}{\partial w_j} = \frac{\partial x(w,y)}{\partial w_j} + \frac{\partial x_i(w,y^*)}{\partial y} \cdot \frac{\partial y(p,w)}{\partial w_j}$$

Rearrange these results to obtain —

$$\frac{\partial y(p,w)/\partial w_i}{\partial y(p,w)/\partial p} = \frac{-\partial x_i(w,y^*)}{\partial y}$$

And —

$$\frac{\partial x_i(p,w)}{\partial w_i} = \frac{\partial x_i(w,y)}{\partial w_i} - \frac{\left(\frac{\partial x_i(p,w)}{\partial p}\right)\left(\frac{\partial x_i(p,w)}{\partial p}\right)}{\underbrace{\partial y(p,w)/\partial p}_{>0}}$$

Which implies $\frac{\partial x_i(p,w)}{\partial w_i} \leq \frac{\partial x_i(w,y^*)}{\partial w_i}$

Or that output — held — constant factor demand is less elastic (implication of Le Chatelier principle)

And finally —

$$\in_{ij}(p,w) = \in_{ij} + \in_{yj}(p,w) \in_{ip}(p,w) / \in_{yp}(p,w)$$

Which can be used to calculate elastistics of substitution, Morishima elasticities, etc

Some examples —

$$\frac{\partial x_i(p,w)}{\partial w_j} = \frac{\partial x_j(p,w)}{\partial w_i} \geq 0 \Rightarrow x_i, x_j \text{ are gross substitutes}$$

We could, however, have, $\frac{\partial x_i(w,y^*)}{\partial y} = \frac{\partial y(p,y)}{\partial w_j} \leq 0$ allowing different signs

So, it is possible to have Hicks-Allen complements but gross substitutes — e.g.

$$\underbrace{\frac{\partial x_i(p,w)}{\partial w_j} = \frac{\partial x_i(w,y)}{\partial w_j}}_{\text{could have diff signs}} + \underbrace{\frac{\partial x_i(p,w)}{\partial y} \cdot \frac{\partial y(p,w)}{\partial w_j}}_{\text{This could change sign}}$$

Short-term vs. long-term distinction —

Everything here is fully analogous to case for cost function —

Define x^2 = fixed inputs (in S.R)

Hotelling's lemma tell us —

$$Y(p, w) = y(p, w^1, x^2(p, w))$$

We know $\Pi(p, w)$ is more convex than $\Pi(p, w, x^2)$ and, when they coincide —

$$\frac{\partial y(p,w)}{\partial p} \geq \frac{\partial y(p,w,x^2(p,w))}{\partial p}$$

(Another implication of Le-Chatelier principle)

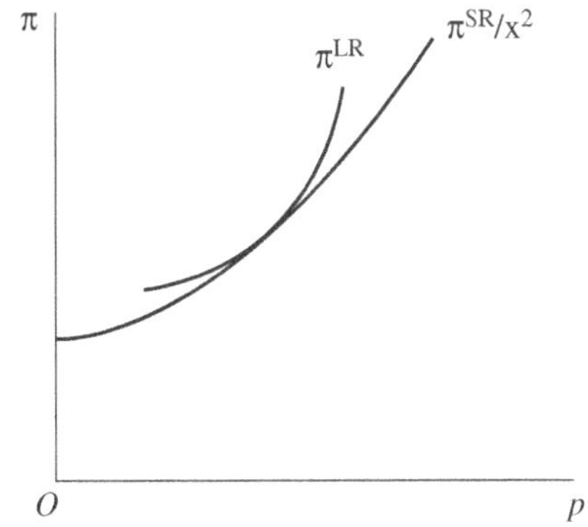

Or, in input space $\frac{\partial x_i(p,w)}{\partial w_i} \le \frac{\partial x_i(p,w,x^2)}{\partial w_i}$

Implications of Homothetic Production

If $f(x)$ is homothetic, we can write —

$$\Pi^*(p, c(w)) \text{ or } c(w)\,\hat{\Pi}(p/c(w))$$

Where Π^* is linearly homogeneous in $p + c(w)$ and $c(w)$ is linearly homogeneous in w.

So — if $f(x)$ is homothetic, profit function is linear homogeneous function of p and a single aggregate input price $c(w)$.

This can be useful in specifying empirical models

Separability

1) Weak separability of Π (p, w) implies —

$$\frac{\partial\left(\frac{\partial\Pi/\partial w_i}{\partial\Pi/\partial w_j}\right)}{\partial w_k} = 0 \qquad \left.\begin{matrix} i,j & \in I \\ k \in k & \end{matrix}\right\} I \neq k$$

This implies derived demand ratios within groups are independent of input prices from other groups

Because — weak separability of Π *(p,w)* does not necessarily imply weak separability of *c*(*w*,*y*) — they have different implications for technology.

2) Strong separability —

$$\frac{\partial\left(\dfrac{\partial\Pi/\partial w_i}{\partial\Pi/\partial w_j}\right)}{\partial w_k}=0 \qquad i\in I \quad j\in J \quad k\neq I\ U\ J$$

An empirical implication of weak separability of profit functions — one can estimate the profit function in terms of aggregate (group-wise) input costs.

Chapter 2

Issues in Production Theory

Flexibility in Estimation

How do we specify a function (cost, profit, etc..) for estimation?

Wider question — how do we measure something that we cannot directly observe?

2 issues — flexibility

— Aggregation

For empirical work, we typically start with some specification of the relationship of interest —

— Cost function
— Profit function
— Production function

We than parameterize the function to reflect our economic theory — we may impose —

— Concavity /convexity
— Separability
— Homogeneity
— Symmetry
— Adding up conditions

These restrictions add information to the problem — and thus reduce estimation problem.

The motion of "flexibility" pertains to the restrictiveness (or lack thereof) of the specification of the technology.

"choice + consequences" of course, any choice of a specification comes with it some consequences.

Example — a cost function linear in prices implies a Leontief production function

To allow this issue, a number of flexible forms have been developed — most based on some form of a power series expansion (e.g. Taylor series)

Consider the primal problem — estimating technology

For n-input case — these are —

n terms of $\partial f/\partial x_i$
n^2 terms of $\partial^2 f/\partial x_i \partial x_j$

But — symmetry of Hessian tells us these are only $n(n-1)\ /_2 + n$ unique terms — which reduces effects to —

$$\frac{1}{2}(n+1)(n+2) \text{ terms}$$

When working with cost or profit functions, we can reduce this further by applying homogeneity and adding up restrictions

We often distinguish functions according to whether they are "linear in parameters" or non-linear

A general linear form —

$$h(z) = \sum_i \alpha_i b_i(z)$$

$b_i(z)$ = known, twice-continuously differentiable function
α_i = parameters to be estimated

Such a form can approximate any arbitrary twice continuously differentiable function

For an arbitrary function $h^*(z)$, we choose parameter such that —

$h^*(z^0) = h(z^0)$ — linear terms
$\forall z\ (z^0) = \forall z\ (z)$ — 1st order Terms
$\forall zz\ (z^0) = \forall zz\ (z)$ — 2nd order Terms

z^0 = point of expansion (note concept of "local" versus "global" flexibility)

These reflect "2nd order approximation".

So — for a functional form that is 2nd — order flexible, when used for a cost function —

Represents cost function in linear terms

Represents ∂_c/w_i = factor demand in 1st order

Represents $\partial_c/w_i^2 = \partial x_i/\partial w_i$ = behavior of factor demands in 2nd order

Consider this as a Taylor's Series Expansion —

Define: $\alpha_1 = \mathrm{h}^*(z^0)$

$$\alpha_i = \partial h^*(z^0)/\partial z_{i-1} \qquad i = 2, \ldots, n+1$$

$$\alpha_j = \partial^z h^*(z^0)/\partial z_v \cdot \partial z_{i-1} \qquad j = n+2, \ldots, \tfrac{1}{2}(n+1)(n+2)$$

And —

$$b_1(\xi^0) = 1$$

$$b_i(\xi^0) = \xi_{i-1} - \xi_{i-1}^0 \; i = 2, \ldots, n+1$$

$$b_j(\xi^0) = \frac{1}{2}\left(\xi_v - \xi_v^0\right)\left(\xi_m - \xi_m^0\right) \quad j = n+2, \ldots, \frac{1}{z}(n+1)(n+2)$$

This yields the familiar Taylor Series form —

$$\hat{h}(z) = \hat{h}(z^0) + \sum_i \left(\frac{\partial \hat{h}(\xi^0)}{\partial \xi_i}\right) z_i \frac{1}{2} \sum_i \sum_j \left(\frac{\partial^2 h(\xi^0)}{\partial \xi_i \partial \xi_j}\right) \xi_i \xi_j + R$$

Form that can be interpreted as 2nd order Taylor series approximations are sometimes called 2nd order numerical approximations.

In practice, we must often use more parsimonious specifications (i.e., fewer parameter) in order to be tractable

Some common flexible functional forms — (from Chambers)

1) Cobb-Donglas

$$h(\xi) = A \cdot \prod_{i=1}^{n} x_i \alpha_i \qquad \alpha_i \geq 0$$

Represents 1st — order Taylor series

2) CES

$$h(\xi) = A\left(\sum_{i=1}^{n} J_i\right)^{1/p}$$

Represents 1st order Taylor series

3) Translog —

$$h(z) = \alpha_0 + \sum_{i=1}^{n} \alpha_1 \ln Z_i + \frac{1}{2}\sum_i \sum_j \alpha_{ij} \ln Z_i \ln Z_j$$

Represents 2nd order Taylor series

4) generalized Leontief (GL)

$$h(z) = \sum_i \sum_j \gamma_{ij} (z_i z_j)^{1/2} \qquad \text{when } \gamma_{ij} = \gamma_{ji}$$

Represents 2nd order Taylor series

5) generalized linear

$$h(\delta) = \sum_i \sum_j B_{ij} Z_i Q_{ij} \left({}^{Z_j}\!/_{Z_i} \right)$$

Represents 2nd order Taylor series

6) generalized Quadratic

$$h(\delta) = \sum_i B_i g_i(z) + \frac{1}{2}\sum_i \sum_j B_{ij} g_i(z_i) g_j(z_j)$$

The Typical Approach

1) We usually work from the dual — with a cost function or profit function
2) Specify a flexible form for the cost (profit function)
3) Apply — Shephard's Lemma — $\partial c/\partial w_i = x_i(w, y)$
   Or — Hotelling's Lemma — $\partial \Pi/\partial w_i = x_i(w, p)$
4) Work with the factor demands in estimable form

It is probably more common to work from cost function, so let's work through several cases for cost function —

1) translog cost function —

$$\ln C = \alpha_0 + \sum_i \alpha_i \ln w_i + \alpha_y \ln y$$
$$+ \frac{1}{2} \sum_i \sum_j \alpha_{ij} \ln w_i \ln w_j$$
$$+ \sum_1 \alpha_{iy} \ln w_i \ln y + \frac{1}{2} \alpha_{yy} \ln y \ln y$$

Restrictions — $\alpha_{ij} = \alpha_{ji}$ (symmetry)

It is common (see, e.g , Berndt + Wood) to impose linear homogeneity by normalizing all prices by a single input price —
eg — $w_1^* = (w_i/w_n)$ {impose within eqn.

Alternatively, it can be imposed directly by —

$$\sum_i \alpha_i = 1 \qquad \text{(Across Eqn)}$$
$$\sum_i \alpha_{ij} = \sum_j \alpha_{ij} = 0 \qquad \text{(Across/within Eqn)}$$
$$\sum \alpha_{iy} = 0 \qquad \text{(Across Eqn)}$$

The translog yields share — dependent factor demands through an application of Shephard's Lemma —

$$S_i = \alpha_i + \sum_{\gamma} \alpha_{ij} \ln w_j + \alpha_{ij} \ln y$$

$$S_i = w_i x_i / C$$

Note — if $\alpha_{ij} = 0\ \forall_i$, the translog implies homothetic technology.

CRS is implied if $\alpha_y = 1$, $\alpha_{iy} = 0\ \forall_i$, and $\alpha_{yy} = 0$

We will talk about aggregation properties below, but note that the translop loses flexibility to capture non-homothetic conditions in aggregate analysis

2) Normalized Quadratic Cost Function (Lau, 1974)

$$C = \alpha_0 + \sum_i x_i w_i + \alpha_y y + \frac{1}{2}\sum_i \sum_j \alpha_{ij} w_i w_j + \sum_i \alpha_{iy} w_i y + \frac{1}{2}\alpha_{yy} y^2,\ \alpha_{ij} = \alpha_{ji}$$

Linear homogeneity is imposed by working with normalized prices $w_i^* = (w_i/w_k)$

This yields input demand equations of the form —

$$x_i = \alpha_i + \sum_j \alpha_{ij} w_j + \alpha_{iy} y$$

This does satisfy aggregation conditions (see below)

3) Generalized Leontief (Diewert and Wales)

$$C = \sum_i \beta_i \omega_i + \sum_i \sum_j \beta_{ij} \omega_i^{1/2} \omega_j^{1/2} y + \beta_{yy} (\Sigma \delta_i \omega_i) y^2$$

where $\beta_{ij} = \beta_{ji}$

This yields factor demand equations of the form

$$X_i = \beta_i + \sum_j \beta_{ij} \omega_i^{-1/2} \omega_j^{1/2} y_k + \beta_{yy} \delta_i y^2$$

CRS is obtained if $\beta_i = 0\ \forall\ i$ and $\beta_{yy} = 0$

If we restrict β_{ij} = 0, the GL becomes quasi-homothetic (but also non-flexible)

4) Generalized McFadden (Diewert and Wales)

$$C = \sum_i \beta_i \omega_i + g(\omega) y_k + \sum_i \beta_{ii} \omega_i y + \beta_{yy} \left(\sum_i \delta_i \omega_i \right) y^2$$

where $g(\omega) = \frac{1}{2} \omega_i^{-1/2} \sum_{i=2}^{n} \gamma_{ij} \omega_i \omega_j$

Symmetry requires $\gamma_{ij} = \gamma_{ji}$
The GM yields factor demand equations

$$X_i = \beta_i + \left(\frac{\partial g(\omega)}{\partial \omega_i} \right) y_k + \beta_{ii} y + \beta_{yy} \delta_i y^2$$

$$\text{where}: \frac{\partial g(\omega)}{\partial \omega} = \frac{1}{2} \omega^2 \sum_{i=2}^{n} \sum_{j=2}^{n} \gamma_{ij} \omega_i \omega_j$$

$$\text{and}: \frac{\partial g(\omega)}{\partial \omega_i} = \sum_{j=2}^{n} \gamma_{ij} \omega^{-1} \omega_j \quad \text{for } i = 2, \ldots, n$$

This is a linear cost function if $\beta_{yy} = 0$
It is quasi-homothetic if $\gamma_i = 0,\ \beta_{ii} = 0 \quad \forall i$

5) CES cost function (Pollak *et al.*)

$$C = \alpha_0 \left(\sum_i \alpha_i \omega_i^{1-\sigma} \right)^{(1/_{1-\sigma})} y^{\alpha y}$$

Or, in logarithmic form

$$In\ C = \alpha_0 + \left(\frac{1}{(1-\sigma)} \right) \text{In} \left(\sum_i \alpha_i \omega_i^{1-\sigma} \right) + \alpha_y \text{ In } y$$

Reduces to Cobb-Douglas as $\sigma \to 1$
This is homothetic cost function.

Aggregation and Specification Issues

The degree to which a specific functional form allows are to consistently aggregate (to work with aggregate — multi-firm data) is also an important issue.

— A fact — our data are almost always subject to some degree of aggregation.
— All of our development and theory to this point applied to cost mini/profit max for a single firm.
— Aggregate "technology" is derived from aggregation across individual firms.
— A nice paper (not in assigned reading) is Kim (2005) — Economic Record — we will follow his presentation.

Assume —

— K technologically independent firms(no externalities)
— Each produces a homogeneous output
— All have identical technology
— Firms $i = 1,..., k,...,$ have production function $y_k = f(X_k)$
— X_k has elements X_{ik} ($i = 1,..., n$ inputs).
— All firms face same input/output prices given by w_i (i = 1,...n).
— Firm K's cost function is dual to production function:

$$C_x(\omega, y_k) = \min_{X_k} \{\omega \cdot X_k : f(X_k) \geq y_k\}$$

— Where $C_k(\cdot)$ has typical properties of linear homogeneity, concavity, etc
— Shephards' lemma applied to individual cost function yields

$$\frac{\partial C_x(\omega, y_k)}{\partial \omega_k} = X_{ik}(\omega, y_k)$$

Define — Aggregate Cost Function

$$C(\omega, y_1, \ldots, y_c) = \sum_k C_k(\omega, y_k)$$

Likewise for inputs: $X_i(\omega, y_1, \ldots, y_k) = \sum_k X_{ik}(\omega, y_k)$

The key question about aggregation relates to how I aggregate $y_1, \ldots, y_k$ across firms.

Q: what conditions must I impart on firms' cost functions such that a solution for an aggregate cost function exists?

Note: since input demands inherit condition from cost function — any aggregation condition that works for cost function carries over to input demands.

Consider an aggregator function: $Y(y_1, \ldots, y_k)$

The problem then becomes one of finding a cost function that permits

$$C(\omega, y_1, \ldots, \text{y}_k) = \text{C}(\omega, Y(\text{y}, \ldots, \text{y}_k))$$

Rules for Consistent Aggregation

*The aggregate cost function exists iff firms cost function is of form

$$C(\omega, y_x) = \alpha_k(\omega) + \beta(\text{y})\text{h}_k(\text{y}_k) \ \{\text{Nonlinear aggregation}\}$$

Or, in special case where $h_k(y_k) = y_k$

$$C(\omega, y_k) = \alpha_k(\omega) + \beta(\omega)\text{y}_k \ \{\text{Linear Aggregation}\}$$

Where: $\left.\begin{array}{l}\alpha_k(\omega)\\ \beta(\omega)\end{array}\right\}$ Linear homogeneous functions of factor prices

Note: $\alpha_k(\omega)$ represents "fixed costs" — does not depend on output (marginal)

$\beta(\omega)$ represents "per unit variable costs"

In case of linear aggregation — the cost function implies quasi- homothetic technologies.

If $\alpha_k(\omega)=0$, technology is homothetic

Using these definitions — consider the aggregate cost function for linear cost

$$C(\omega, Y(y,\ldots,y_x)) = \sum_k X_k(\omega) + \beta(\omega)\cdot\sum_k y_k$$

where $Y=\sum_k y_k$

Note: We can also work with "average" or representative cost function $\overline{\alpha_k(\omega)+\beta(\omega)}\bar{y}$

Aggregate Cost Function for Non-Linear Case

$$C(\omega, Y(y_1,\ldots,y_k)) = \sum_k \alpha_k(\omega) + \beta(\omega)\sum_k h_k(y_k)$$

$$\text{Or that } Y = h^{-1}\left(\sum_k h_k(y_k)\right)$$

$$\text{(may not be equal to } \sum_k y_k\text{)!}$$

*A key result-aggregate cost depends on the distribution of output across firms.

Now, let's consider a more general form

$$C(\omega, y_1,\ldots,y_k) = C(\omega, Y_1(y_1,\ldots,y_k))\ldots, Y_m(y_1,\ldots,y_k)$$

where $Y_m(m=1,\ldots,m)$ is an output aggregator function

It can be shown that this new regular form exists

If — the firms' cost functions can be written as:

Generalized aggregation $\quad C_k(\omega, y_k) = \alpha_k(\omega) + \sum_m \beta_m(\omega)h_{xm}(y_k)$

where: $\left.\begin{matrix}\alpha_k(\omega)\\ \beta_m(\omega)\end{matrix}\right\}$ linear, homogeneous concave functions

We typically assume that $M < k$ (# aggregation function is less than number of firms)

One example of such a cost function —

$$C_k(\omega, y_k) = \alpha_k(\omega) + \beta_1(\omega) y_k + \beta_2(\omega) h_k(y_k)$$

which is a hybrid of a linear (β_1 term) and nonlinear (β_2 term) cost function

If individual cost function looks like this, the aggregate cost function is —

$$\begin{aligned} & C(\omega, Y_1(y_1, \dots, y_k) \dots, Y_2(y_1, \dots, y_k)) \\ & = \sum_k \alpha_k(\omega) + \beta_1(\omega) \sum_k y_k + \beta_2(\omega) \sum_k h_k(y_k) \\ & \text{where } Y_1 = \sum_k y_k, Y_2 = h^{-1} \left[\sum_k h_k(y_k) \right] \end{aligned}$$

This presents exact, consistent aggregation

An example = the Box — Cost transformation —

$$h_k(y_k) = \begin{cases} (y_k^{\lambda} - 1)/\lambda & \text{for } \lambda \neq 0 \\ \ln y_k \quad as \ \lambda \to 0 \end{cases}$$

Use this for individual cost function

$$\begin{aligned} C_k(\omega, y_k) &= \alpha_k^*(\omega) + \beta_1(\omega) y_k + \beta_2^*(\omega) y_k^{\lambda} \quad \text{for } \lambda \neq 0 \\ &= \alpha_k(\omega) + \beta_1(\omega) y_k + \beta_2 \ln y_k \qquad \lambda \to 0 \end{aligned}$$

where $\alpha_k^* = \alpha_k(\omega) - \beta_2(\omega)/\lambda$

$\beta_2^* = \beta_2(\omega)/\lambda$

(Note, If $\lambda = 1$, everything becomes linear)

Using this aggregate cost function becomes,

$$C(\omega, Y(.)...) = \sum_k \alpha_k^*(\omega) + \beta_1(\omega)\sum_k y_k$$
$$+ \beta_2^*(\omega)\sum_k h_k(y_k^\lambda) \qquad \lambda \neq 0$$

and $\sum_k \alpha_k(\omega) + \beta_1(\omega)\sum_k y_k + \beta_2(\omega)\sum_k \ln y_k$ for $\lambda \to 0$

for $\lambda \to 0$ $C(\omega_1\, y_1(.), y_2(.))$ implies

$$Y_1 = \sum_k y_k$$

$$Y_2 = \exp\left(\sum_k \ln y_k\right)$$

for $\lambda \neq 0$ $\quad C(\omega_1 Y_1(.), Y_2(.))$ implies

$$Y_1 = \sum_k y_k$$

$$Y_2 = \left[\sum_k y_k^\lambda\right]^{1/k}$$

*— So, if individual cost function looked like what we specified above (Box-Cox), the aggregate cost function must look like this — with these exact terms

If I used in $\ln \sum_k y_k$ instead of $\sum_k \ln y_k$ — I get bias

Now, let's returns to former examples and examine whether they permit exact linear or nonlinear aggregation

Remember —

Exact linear: $C(\omega, y_1,\ldots,y_k) = \sum \alpha_k(\omega) + \beta(\omega)\sum y_k$
Exact nonlinear: $C(\cdot) = \sum_k \alpha_k(\omega^k) + \beta(\omega)\sum_k h_k(y_k^k)$

Exact Generalized Aggregation

$$C(\cdot)=\sum_k \alpha_k(\omega)+\sum_k\left(\sum_m \beta_m(\omega)h_{xm}(y_k)\right)$$

$$\text{Translog: } \quad \text{In}\, C_k=\alpha_k+\sum_i \alpha_i \,\text{In}\omega_i+\alpha_y \,\text{In}\, y_k$$
$$+\frac{1}{2}\sum_i\sum_j \alpha_{ij}\,\text{In}\,\omega_i\,\text{In}\,\omega_j$$
$$+\sum_i \alpha_{iy}\,\text{In}\,\omega_i\,\text{In}\, y_k+\frac{1}{2}\alpha_{yy}(\text{In}\, y_k)^2$$

Can we write this in a form to allow exact nonlinear aggreagation?

$$\beta(\omega)=\exp\left[\alpha_0+\frac{1}{2}\sum_i\sum_j \ln\omega_i \ln\omega_j\right], \text{ and}$$

$$h_k(y_k)=\exp\left[\alpha_y \ln y_k+\frac{1}{2}\alpha_{yy}(\ln y_k)^2\right]$$

This only allows consistent aggregation of —
$\alpha_{iy}=0 \quad \forall i \quad \Rightarrow$ nonlinear homothetic technology

Note problem is term $=\left(\sum_i \alpha_{iy}\ln\omega_i \ln y_k\right)$

So translog only allows consistent nonlinear aggregations if technology is homothetic — so not very good aggregation

Consider another functional form —
Normalized Quadratic

$$C_k=\alpha_0+\sum_i \alpha_i\omega_i+\alpha_y y_k+\frac{1}{2}\sum_i\sum_j a_{ij}\omega_i\omega_j+\sum_i \alpha_{iy}\omega_i y_k+\frac{1}{2}a_{yy}y_k^z$$

It is pretty obvious that the NQ satisfies generalized consistent aggregation without further restrictions because —

$$\alpha(\omega) = \alpha_0 + \sum_i \alpha_i \omega_i + \frac{1}{2}\sum_i \sum_j \alpha_{ij}\omega_i \omega_j$$

$$\beta_1(\omega) = \alpha_y + \sum_i \alpha_i \omega_i.$$

$$\beta_2(\omega) = \frac{1}{2} a_{yy}$$

with $h_k(y_k) = yx^2$

So — NQ is more attractive on grounds of aggregation than is translog

Consider one more —

generalized Leontief —

$$C_k = \sum_i \beta_i \omega_i + \sum_i \sum_j b_{ij} \omega_i^{1/2} \omega_j^{1/2} y_k + \beta_{yy} \left(\sum_i \delta_i \omega_i \right)_{y_k}^{\lambda}$$

It clearly satisfies generalized aggregation.

Note, if $\beta_{yy} = 0$, we have:

$$\alpha(\omega) = \sum_i b_i \omega_i$$

$$\beta_1(\omega) = \sum_i \sum_j \beta_{1j} \omega_i^{1/2} \omega_j^{1/2}$$

⇒ Linear form — satisfied linear aggregates

A key finding of Kim's paper — translog does not have good aggregation properties since exact aggregation of translog requires homothetic technologies — a strong assumption.

Chapter 3

Econometric Issues in Applied Demand Analysis

Regularity conditions —

If conditions involving "curvature" that estimates of one demand system should satisfy —

1) Quasi-Concavity (negativity — S_{ij} should be negative semi-definite, etc.).
2) Monotonicity — (nonsatiatian) — generally expressed in terms that predicted quantities or budget shares should always be positive

Our other restrictions (adding-up, homogeneity etc.) are straightforward to impose / test — they involve direct parametric restrictions

These curvature conditions are not so straightforward to impose or test as they involve inequality restrictions.

For example — recall the Rotterdam model —

$$\omega_i l \ln yi = \beta_1 l \ln Q + \sum_i C_{ik} l \ln p_i$$

Quasi-concavity requires that the substitution matrix C — with elements given by C_{ix} — must be negative semi definite.

Among other things (involving cross-terms) this requires the diagonal elements to be negative — $C_{ii} < 0 \quad \forall i$.

How would one impose this? It is indeed difficult using parametric restrictions — but there are two common methods to doing so

Imposing Curvature

1) A Bayesian Approach — involving Monte–Carlo Integration (attributable to Klock and van Dijk (1978) and Geweke (1986, 88, 89)
Consider a AIDS demand system — AIDS

$$\omega_i = \alpha_i + \sum_j \gamma_{ij} \ln p_j + \beta_i \ln y_i$$

Quasi-Concavity of preferences requires the matrix C to be negative semi definite, where typical terms is ⇒

$$C_{ij} = \gamma_{ij} + \beta_i \beta_j \ln\left(\frac{x}{P}\right) - \omega_i \delta_{ij} + \omega_i \omega_j$$

Note — this does not say that γ (γ_{ij} elements, must be negative — semi definite — though this is sufficient but not necessary condition for concavity

Note — requires, γ_{ij} elements to satisfy concavity "over restricts" the estimates — too strong.

(Exposition uses AIDS demand model. Carries over completely to translog case)

How can we test/require this to hold?

Lets view the estimation problem in Bayesian terms —

Say θ = parameter set to be estimated. We believe θ should lie is a certain region suggested by our theory.

So — we have a prior about θ.

Recall Bayes Theorem — of we have —

A prior — $p(\theta)$

A likelihood function based on data — $y = L(\theta)$y

Bayes Theorem tells us that a posterior distribution for θ (beliefs involving are prior — adjusted for what we see in the data) is given by —

$$f(\theta, y) \propto \rho(\theta) \angle(\theta / y)$$

The posterior summarizes all of our information about θ — including what we believed beforehand — the prior — and what the data tell us — the likelihood function.

An analytical solution yielding mean values of θ from the posterior — which would represent our parameter estimates is very difficult as it involves high -ordered integrals —

For example —

Suppose you have a K-dimensional parameter matrix θ — your prior tells you that only certain region (denote as $\theta \in D$) and valid — in a large sample — you assume $\theta \sim N(\hat{\theta}, \hat{\Sigma})$, How do you obtain posterior estimates? must integrate —

$$E(\theta) = \int_{\theta x \in D} \cdots \int_{\theta x \in D} \theta N(\hat{\theta}, \hat{\Sigma})\, d\theta_1 \cdots d\theta_n$$

The calculation is infeasible in all but most trivial cases.

A much simpler solution — use Monte–Carlo Integration to estimate restricted θ.

Integration by Monte–Carlo involves using random draws to build/ measure a distribution.

How would we do it — generate a large N (5000 e.g.) number of values of θ_i, from the distribution $\theta \sim N(\hat{\theta}, \hat{\Sigma})$ and estimate

$$\bar{\theta} = \frac{\sum_{i-1}^{N} \theta_i}{N}$$

Consider now the case where one wants to restrict θ to take only certain values $\theta \in D$ (e.g. $\theta \leq 0$ only).

How could we do it? — generate large number of θ_i — keep only those that satisfy the restriction — estimate restricted θ as mean of this subsample

$$\hat{\theta}_D = \frac{\Sigma \theta_i^D}{n}$$

Where n = # replicated satisfying $\theta \in D$

In large sample problem where we start with maximum likelihood estimates, if cross equation covariance matrix is known with certainly — $\theta \sim N(\hat{\theta}, \hat{\Sigma})$.

So draw θ from multivariable normal —
The approach is —

1) Estimate parameters of model — $\beta_i, \gamma_{ij}, \alpha_i$ in case of AIDS model, along with their covariance matrix — use standard ML restriction to get $\hat{\theta}.\hat{\Sigma}$
2) Treat these as parameters of posterior in case of no restriction (different priors).
3) Now — draw random sample of parameters from $N(\hat{\theta}, \hat{\Sigma})$

Geweke gives techniques for doing so — it is relatively simple —

$$Take\ p = chol(\hat{\Sigma}) - \text{ choleski decomp}$$

such that $p'p = \hat{\Sigma}$
generate e =a k-dimensional vector of draw from standard normal

$$\theta_i = \hat{\theta} + pe'$$

(Geweke recommends speeding up the process by also taking $\theta_i = \hat{\theta} - p'e$ since deviations should be symmetric — calls this antithetic acceleration).

4) For each θ_i replication — evaluate the condition underlying the test — for example in case of concavity, in AIDS model check to see if $C(\theta_i)$ is negative semidefinite — if so — keep θ_i, if not reject θ_i.
5) Do this large number of times — sorting replications that satisfy restrictions from those that do not
6) Estimate restricted $\bar{\theta}$ by using average of n subset of replications is restricted space D.

$$\bar{\theta} = \frac{\sum_{i=1}^{n} \theta_i}{n} \text{ and } \frac{\sum \left(\theta_i - \bar{\theta}\right)^2}{n} = \sqrt{\theta}$$

7) Proportion of observation satisfying restrictions is estimate of p-value of test of restriction $p = n/N$

Now we assumed that $\hat{\Sigma}$ was known rather then estimated — by using a multivariable normal rather than *t* distribution.

This is not entirely consistent with exact position since draws should come from *t* - distribution.

Chalfant *et al.* describe how this approach can be amended in order to obtain exact results. It is very common to just use the multivariate normal in emprical work.

Chalfant *et al.* apply this to Canadian meat demand — impose monotonicity and concavity.

One potential problem — if restrictions are strongly violated by data — may be hard to get replication that ever satisfy restrictions.

The Ryan + Wales Approach to Imposing Concavity

Ryan + Wales JBES (1998) —

A simple approach that really has been around for some time. This has been used to impose positive semi-definite parameter matrix in multivariate GARCH models.

The idea is simple — if you require some matrix S to be negative semidefinite — use its — cholesky decomposition to construct a matrix that must be n.s.d. by construction

i.e. — example — (A'A) — where A = Chol(s)

For example — in AIDS where p* is non linear model —

$$s_i = \alpha_i + \Sigma\gamma_{ij} \text{In}\, p_j + \beta_i \text{In}\, y$$

Concavity requires that the slutsky substitution matrix must be negative semidefinite.

In AIDS model the i, j^{th} element of this matrix is given by

$$S_{ij} = \gamma_{ij} + \beta_i\beta_j \ln(x/p_x) - \omega_i\delta_i + \omega_i\omega_j$$

(Note different form of this in Ryan + Wales — expressed for $p^* = 1, x = 1$) → Assume $\alpha_0 = 0$

$$S_{ij} = \gamma_{ij} - \omega_i\delta_{ij} + \omega_i\omega_j$$

Imposing concavity is accomplished by setting
$S = -(\mathrm{A}'\mathrm{A})$ and estimating elements of A_{ij}
So — set $S = -(\mathrm{A}'\mathrm{A})$ and solve for γ_{ij}

$$\gamma_{ij} = -(\mathrm{A}'\mathrm{A})_{ij} - \alpha\delta_{ij} + \alpha.X_j$$

This is used in place of γ_{ij}, in estimation that is, element of A_{ij} are estimated rather than γ_{ij}.

An easier problem the Rotterdam model

$$\omega_i d \ln y_i = \beta_i d \ln Q + \sum_j C_{ij} d \ln p_i$$

Concavity requires C to the negative semidefinite. But we will not estimate C directly but will estimate $A_{ij} - where - (\mathrm{A}'\mathrm{A}) = \mathrm{C}$ — and recover C from this.

Suppose we have a demand system of $k = 4$ goods what will A look like

A = Chol (C) {IML uses "HALF (C)"}

$$A = \begin{bmatrix} a_{11} & a_{12} & a_{13} & a_{14} \\ 0 & a_{22} & a_{23} & a_{24} \\ 0 & 0 & a_{33} & a_{34} \\ 0 & 0 & 0 & a_{44} \end{bmatrix}$$

So — the elements of C will be like →

$$-(\mathrm{A}'\mathrm{A}) = -1 * \begin{bmatrix} a_{11}^2 & a_{11}a_{12} & a_{11}a_{13} & a_{11}a_{14} \\ ,, & a_{12}^2 + a_{22}^2 & a_{13}a_{12} + a_{22}a_{23} & a_{12}a_{14} + a_{22}a_{21} \\ ,, & ,, & a_{13}^2 + a_{23}^2 + a_{33}^2 & a_{13}a_{14} + a_{23}a_{24} + a_{33}a_{34} \\ ,, & ,, & ,, & a_{14}^2 + a_{24}^2 + a_{34}^2 + a_{44}^2 \end{bmatrix}$$

So — $C_{11} = -a_{11}^2$

$$C_{12} = C_{21} = -a_{11}a_{12}$$

$$\vdots$$

$$C_{34} = C_{43} = -(a_{13}a_{14} + a_{23}a_{24} + a_{33}a_{34})$$

So — its a simple matter to express the model in these terms — thereby imposing concavity by construction.

Ryan and Wales develop this method for several common demand systems — the normalized quadratic, AIDS, and linear translog.

Note: these are problems in making inferences about constrained parameters in these cases — as they may be close to boundaries.

This is a topic of current research in econometrics.

Autocorrelation in Singular Systems of Equations

Basic approach

Consider share equation from demand system —

$$\omega_{it} = f(\theta, X_t) + \varepsilon_t$$

Where $\sum_i \omega_{it} = 1$

$$\varepsilon_t \sim N(0, \hat{\Sigma})$$

The fact that $\Sigma\omega_{it} = 1$ at every t means that Σ is singular.

We address this by omitting one equation and recovering estimates using adding up restrictions.

We have not thought much about time series properties of wt (or ε_t).

We have made a vague reference to the famous result of Barten (1969).

Invariance — if we use max, likelihood estimation procedures (or equivalently, iterated SUR) — our results will be invariant with respect to which equation we delete (because of singularity of Σ).

Now — consider what happens when ε_t in autocorrelated.

We can write this as —

$$\varepsilon_t = R\varepsilon_{t-1}$$

Where R is an $n \times n$ parameter matrix.

A very famous paper by Bendt and Savin (1975) shows that the invariable property generally breaks down.

In terms of estimating parameters of the model, θ, we could rewrite the model as —

$$y_t = f(\theta, X_t) + R(y_{t-1} - f(\theta, X_{t-1})) + V_t$$

And estimate using standard M.L.

In the familiar case where R is diagonal — Bendt and Savin show that invariance holds only if every equation has an identical autocorrelation term — i.e., if R is —

$$R = \begin{bmatrix} \rho & & & 0 \\ & \rho & & \\ & & \ddots & \\ 0 & & & \rho \end{bmatrix} \leftarrow All\ \rho\text{'s same}$$

This does not allow for lagged errors in the equation to exert an effect (through cross — equation autocorrelation) on another equation.

It is very common to assume a common ρ for each equation and estimate this in order to correct for any residual autocorrelation.

Moschini & Moro (1994) describe some methods for pursuing more general forms of autocorrelation in singular demand systems which maintain the invariance property. Holt has presented a way of getting more parsimonious specifications by applying rank reduction techniques of R.

Moschini and Moro Approach

A general approach to correcting for autocorrelation is systems of singular equation while maintaining adding up.

This extends Bendt + Savin method of using the same autocorrelation parameter for each equation.

Consider the model —

$$y_t = f(\theta, \varepsilon_t) + V_t$$

$$\Sigma y_t = 1 \Rightarrow \Sigma V_t = 0 \qquad \forall t$$

Assumes 1st order auto regressive process

$$V_t = RV_{t-1} + \varepsilon_t$$

Singularity requires all columns of R to add to the same constant
Dropping one equation — we write this as

$$V_t^n = \bar{R}^n V_{t-1}^n + \varepsilon_t^n$$

We rewrite the system as

$$y_t^n = f^n(V_t, \theta) + \bar{R}^n \left[y_{t-1}^n - f^n(\theta, \varepsilon_{t-1}) + \varepsilon_f^n \right]$$

M & M show that, if R is assumed to be singular, symmetric, dependent on only R parameters — it can be written as

$$R = \wedge - \frac{\lambda\lambda'}{\Sigma^n \lambda_s}$$

$$\textit{where} \qquad \wedge = \begin{bmatrix} \lambda_1 & & 0 \\ & \ddots & \\ 0 & & \lambda_n \end{bmatrix} \qquad \textit{and} \quad \lambda = \begin{bmatrix} \lambda_1 \\ \vdots \\ \lambda_n \end{bmatrix}$$

Which implies —

$$\bar{R}_{11} = \lambda_1 - \frac{\lambda_i(\lambda_1 - \lambda_n)}{\Sigma_i \lambda_s} \qquad i = 1$$

$$\bar{R}_{ij} = -\frac{\lambda_i(\lambda_j - \lambda_n)}{\Sigma_s \lambda_s} \qquad i \neq j$$

See application to AIDS model

Chapter 4

Multiproduct Technologies

Of course, most commodities are produced in connection with others.

This can raise substantial complications.

We are used to considering this in terms of a production possibility function.

$$\text{Slope} \quad PPF = MRTS = -\frac{dy_1}{dy_2} = -\frac{f_2}{f_1}$$

PPF is a concave function of either output:

$$d\frac{\left(-\frac{dy_1}{dy_2}\right)}{dy_2} < 0$$

We typically consider things in terms of a production possibilities set $T(\cdot)$ —

$T\ (x, y)$ = set of all x (inputs) — y (outputs) combinations that are technically feasible.

Properties of T

1) T is nonempty
2) T is a closed set

3) T is convex
4) *if* $(x, y) \in T,\ X' \geq X \Rightarrow (x', y) \in T$ (free disposability of X)
5) *if* $(x, y) \in T,\ y' \leq y \Rightarrow (x, y') \in T$ (free disposability of Y)
6) For any finite x, T is bounded from above
7) $(x, Om) \in T$ but *if* $y \geq 0, (On, y) \notin T$ (Weak essentiality)

   Note — all are very similar to what was encountered before.
   Define: Input requirement set $V(y) = \{X : (x, y) \in T\}$
   Same as before, except now y is a vector of outputs
   We need a multivariable generalization of production function —
   Many ways to do this, one is to consider
   "Producible Output Set" $y(x) = \{y : (x, y) \in T\}$

Producible Output Set

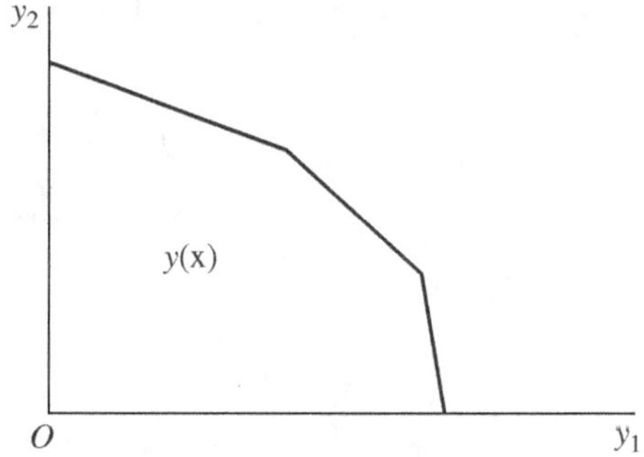

Properties of $y(x)$ (carry over completely)

1) $y(x)$ is nonempty and closed
2) *if* $y \in y(x), y' \leq y$, then $y \in y(x)$
   likewise, *if* $X' \geq x$ then $y(x') \geq y(x)$
3) $y(x)$ is convex
4) $y(x)$ bounded above for finite x
5) *if* $y = 0$, $y \in y(\text{On})$; $Om \in y(x)$

Multiproduct Definition of CRS

For $(x,y) \in T$, T has CRS if

$(\theta x, \theta y) \in \mathrm{T}$ for $\theta > 0$

Implies all isoquants are evenly spaced (for scalar θ) and are parallel.
Deriving a production function form T —
$f(x) = \max\{y : (x,y) \in T\} = \max\{y : y \in T\}$

Multiproduct Indirect Objective Functions —
Multioutputs Cost Function — $v(y)$ —
These conditions carry over largely intact

— Shephard's Lemma applies (with differentiability)
— Comparative statics applies
— Homogeneity carries over
— $\dfrac{\partial^2 C}{\partial \omega_i \partial y_j} = \dfrac{\partial^2 C}{\partial y_j \partial \omega_i}$

It is also often convenient to consider multioutput case in terms of revenue functions —

Revenue function: $R(p, x) = \max\{p.y : y \in y(x), \rho > 0\}$
Properties —

1) $R(p,\mathrm{x}) \geq 0$
2) $if\ p' \geq p\ R(p',x) \geq R(p,x)$
3) $R(t_p, x) = t \cdot R(p,x)$ (homogeneous of degree)
4) $R(p, x)$ is convex and continuous in p
5) $if\ X' \geq X\ R(p,x') \geq R(p,x)$

A variant of the Hotelling's lemma applies to the revenue function known as

Samuelson — McFadden lemma

$$y_i(p \cdot x) = \frac{\partial R(p,x)}{\partial p_i}$$

Multiproduct Profit Function

3 equivalent versions —

$$\pi(p,\omega) = \max_{y,x}\{p.y - \omega x : (x,y) \in T, \omega, p > 0\}$$

$$\max_{y,x}\{p.y - C(\omega, y) : \omega, p > 0\}$$

$$\max_{y,x}\{R(p,y) - \omega \cdot \mathrm{x} : \omega, p > 0\}$$

Properties of multiinput profit function

1) $\pi(p,\omega) \geq 0$
2) $if\ p' \geq p,\ \pi(p',\omega) \geq \pi(p,\omega)$
3) $if\ \omega' \geq \omega,\ \pi(p,\omega') \leq \pi(p,\omega)$
4) $\pi(p,\omega)$ is convex and continuous in all arguments
5) $\pi(t \cdot p, t \cdot \omega) = t \cdot \pi(p,\omega)$ (linear homogenous)
6) There exist fixed vectors such that $(\bar{y},\bar{x}),(\hat{y},\hat{x})$
   $\pi(p,\omega) \geq p \cdot \bar{y} - \omega \cdot \bar{x}$ and $\pi(p,\omega) \leq p \cdot y' - \omega \cdot \hat{x}$

This is used in demonstrating some duality results
Another version of Hotelling's Lemma

$$\frac{\partial \pi(p,\omega)}{\partial p_i} = y_i(p,\omega)$$

$$\frac{\partial \pi(p,\omega)}{\partial \omega_i} = -x_i(p,\omega)$$

Comparative statics —

$$(p' - p)(y' - y) - (\omega' - \omega)(x' - x) \geq 0$$

Called "fundamental Inequality of Profit Max"
Put differently — $\Delta p \cdot \Delta y - \Delta\omega \cdot \Delta x \geq 0$

$if\ \Delta p > 0 \Rightarrow \Delta y > 0$

$if\ \Delta\omega > 0 \Rightarrow \Delta x < 0$

This implies decomposition results of the form

$$\frac{\partial y_i(p,\omega)}{\partial p_j} = \frac{\partial y_i(p,x)}{\partial p_j} + \sum_{v=1}^{n} \frac{\partial y_i(p,x)}{\partial x_v} \cdot \frac{\partial x_v(p,x)}{\partial p_j}$$

$$\frac{\partial y_i(p,\omega)}{\partial \omega_x} = \sum_{v=1}^{n} \frac{\partial y_i(p,x)}{\partial x_v} \cdot \frac{\partial x_v(p,x)}{\partial x_x}$$

Likewise for factor demands —

$$\frac{\partial x_i(p,\omega)}{\partial p_j} = \sum_{v=1}^{n} \frac{\partial x_i(\omega,y)}{\partial y_v} \cdot \frac{\partial y_v}{\partial p_j}$$

$$\frac{\partial x_i(p,\omega)}{\partial \omega_x} = \frac{\partial x_i(\omega,y)}{\partial \omega_x} + \sum_{v=1}^{m} \frac{\partial x_i(\omega,y)}{\partial y_v} \cdot \frac{\partial y_v}{\partial \omega_x}$$

The Structure of Multioutput Technologies —
Restrictions in the definition of T(.) —
"Jointness"—

3 Types: 1) Technical jointness — input jointness — ouput jointness } Mainly concerned with this

2) Physical jointness
— distinction not critical

3) Behavioral jointness

Output Separability — Replace vector of output with single output index $(x, y(y)) \in \mathrm{T}$

$\Rightarrow (x, y) \in \mathrm{T}$

1) Nonjoint in inputs —
T(·) is nonjoint in inputs if,
for every $(x, y) \in T$ there exists vectors
$X' \geq 0$ such that

$$y_i \leq f^i(x^i),\ \Sigma X^i \leq X \quad i = 1, \ldots, m$$

where $f'(\cdot)$ is a production function that satisfies all the usual restrictions.

$\Rightarrow$ Each output has its own production function

2) Nonjoint in outputs —
   T(·) is nonjoint in outputs if, for every $(x, y) \in T$ there exists

$$X^i \geq g^i(y^i), \sum_{i=1}^{n} y^i \geq y, \quad i = 1, \ldots, n$$

   Where $g^i(y^i)$ is non empty, producible set
   Example is where one input is seperated into a number of outputs — eg. a cow (input) is repeated into meat, leather, offal
3) A third type of nonjointness arises when production proceeds in stages, as on a production line. This is called Kohli- Output case nonjointness. This is special case of Leontief technologies — see Chambers for discussion.

An Analogous Definition (from Lau)

* Production function is nonjoint in inputs if there exists individual production function such that

$$y_i = f_i(x_i, \ldots, x_{im}) \text{ and } X_j = \sum_i X_{ij} \text{ implies}$$
$$F(y_1, \ldots, y_m, \quad x_1, \ldots, x_n) = 0$$

* Production function is nonjoint in outputs if there exists individual input requirement function such that

$$X_j = g_j(y_{1j}, \ldots, y_{mj}) \text{ and } y_i - \sum_j y_{ij} \text{ implies}$$
$$F(y_1, \ldots, y_m, \quad x_1, \ldots, x_n) = 0$$

Causes of Jointness

Technical Interactions & Economics of Scope —

Economics of scope — something in production technology makes it cheaper (more expensive) to produce goods jointly.

Allocable Fixed Inputs

Allocable input — can distinguish how much *X* goes to produce each *Y*

Well known paper by Shumwas, Pope, and Mark (AJAE 1984) showed that jointness in production can be caused by presence of an allocable fixed input —

Consider Z output case, with one variable input and one fixed allocable input —

$$y_i = f_i(x_i, z_i) \quad i = 1,2$$

X_i = Variable input
Z_i = fixed, allocable input
{Nonjoint in inputs

$$z_1 + z_2 = \bar{z}_1 = \textit{Stock of fixed input}$$

We can rearrange this system of two equations as follows —

$$x_1 = f_1 x_1^{-1}(y_1, z_1)$$
$$z_2 = f_2 z_2^{-1}(y_2, x_2, z)$$
$$z_1 = \bar{z} - z_2 = \bar{z} - f_2 z_2^{-1}(y_2, x_2, \bar{z})$$

Now consider $\dfrac{\partial^2 x_1}{\partial y_1 \partial y_2}$

In rule for technology to be nonjoint, this must be zero —

$$\frac{\partial^2 x_1}{\partial y_1 \partial y_2} = \frac{\partial\left(\partial x_1/\partial y_1\right)}{\partial y_2}$$
$$= \left[\frac{\partial\left(\partial x_1/\partial y_1\right)}{\partial z_1}\right]\left(\frac{\partial z_1}{\partial y_2}\right)$$
$$= \underbrace{\left[\frac{\partial\left(\partial x_1/\partial y_1\right)}{\partial z_1}\right]}_{A}\underbrace{\left(-\frac{\partial z_2}{\partial y_2}\right)}_{B}$$

In rules for this to be zero — we must have A = 0

Only if marginal requirement of variable input is independent of fixed input (A = 0) will technology be nonjoint

So — strong condition is required for nonjointness when there is an allocable fixed input.

Chapter 5

Producer Choice Under Uncertainty

Everything to this point has assumed perfect information — of course this does not apply —

A good general (simple) review of issues is provided by Buschena & Zilberman (1994).

Review —

A few competing paradigms —

1) Expected utility (the stalwart approach)
2) Generalization of EU
   — prospect theory
   — disappointment aversion
   — safety rules
3) State contingency (Chambers & Quiggen)

99% of existing empirical (and theoretical) analysis is based on EU theory

Buschena and Zilberman (BZ) define 2 types of EU theory.

Normative EU — (positive — expansion to distributional and equity views)

Based on simple expected value maximization

$$E(x,p) = \sum_i x_i p(x_i)$$

where X = outcome, p(.) = probability

Since utility is not necessarily, linear in wealth we often use —

$$Eu(x,p) = \sum_i V(\omega_i)p(\omega_i)$$
$$= \sum_i V(\omega_0 + x_i)p(x_i)$$

Where X_i = change in wealth

ω_0 = initial wealth

A few important (though standard) concepts — certainty equivalence and the risk premium — consider a lottery of payouts X_i, with prob = p(·)

The certainty equivalent c(p) is the value of certain payment that makes agent indifferent between payment and lottery — where x = outcome P(.) = probability

$$U(c(p)) = \sum_i u(x_i)p(x_i)$$

Consider expected value of risky outcome

$$\overline{X} = \Sigma p_i(x_i) \cdot x_i$$

If we consider difference in expected utility of an average and certainty equivalent, we get —

Risk premium $= \pi(p) = u(\overline{x}) - c(p)$

Consider standard picture for concave utility

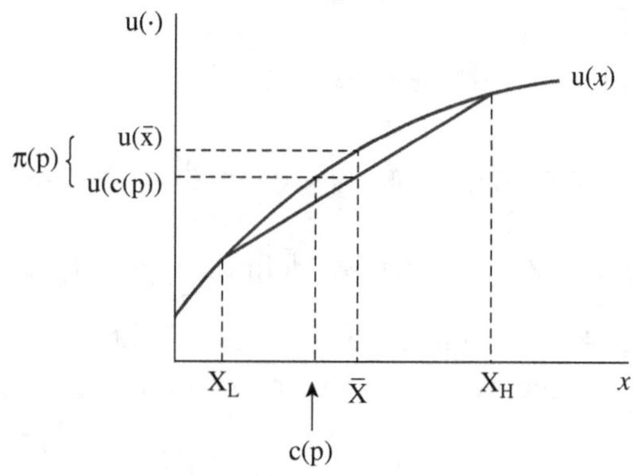

$p(x) = x_L = \frac{1}{2}$
$p(x) = x_H = \frac{1}{2}$

Measures of Risk Aversion
These mainly derive from Arrow and Pratt

1) Absolute Risk Aversion Coefficient (R_A) —

$$R_A = -\frac{U''(x)}{U'(x)}$$

2) A relative version is similar to an elasticity

$$R_R = \left[\frac{X \cdot U''(x)}{U'(x)}\right]$$

3) Partial Risk Aversion measures — a "before and after" comparison —

$$R_R = -\frac{U''(X + \Delta X) \cdot X}{U'(x)}$$

X = initial wealth
$X + \Delta X$ = final wealth

How do risk preferences change as income/wealth change?
This is a very important distinction —

$\frac{\partial R_A}{\partial \omega} < 0 \Rightarrow$ Decreasing Absolute Risk Aversion
$> 0 \Rightarrow$ increasing Absolute Risk Aversion

$\frac{\partial R_A}{\partial \omega} < 0$ is a common assumption and drives a lot of policy questions of the day —

In doing analytical work, we typically need to adopt some specific representations of risk preferences — $U(\omega)$

Some comments regarding practicality —
$U(\omega)$ should have

1) simplicity
2) $u' > 0, u'' < 0$
3) DARA or CARA — $\dfrac{\partial R_A}{\partial \omega} \leq 0$
4) Non-decreasing relative risk aversion —

$$\frac{\partial R_C}{\partial \omega} \geq 0$$

If R_R is constant, should be close to one

Some Specific Functions

1) Quadratic — $u(\omega) = a + b\omega - c\omega^2$
   Implies increasing absolute risk aversion
2) Cobb–Douglass $u(\omega) = A\omega^{\alpha}$ $0 < \alpha < 1$
   Implies constant R_R and decreasing R_A
   Problems — 1) $R_R = 1 \Rightarrow \alpha = 0$
   2) Complex to take expectations
3) Logarithmic — $u(\omega) = \ln \omega$
   Implies constant R_R with $R_R = 1$ and DARA
   Can be hard to work with.
4) Exponential utility function — $u(\omega) = 1 - e^{-r\omega}$
   Has CARA with $R_A(\omega) = \gamma$
   Easy to apply

Mean-Variance Functions

Suppose $\omega \sim N(\mu, \sigma^2)$

Any solution that maximizes $\left(\mu - \frac{1}{2}\gamma \cdot \sigma^2\right)$ also maximizes $E(\mathrm{u}(\omega))$ when utility is exponential.

Further — max of linear function of mean and variance is equivalent to expected utility max.

Stochastic Dominance

"Mean preserving spread" concept — idea is to compare choices with same mean and argue that risk averse agents prefer choices with less mass in tails.

Mean preserving spread = transformation of pdf to keep means constant. The transformation shifts mass from center to tails

Def: $F(y)$ is mean measuring spread of $G(y)$, if

$$\int_{-\infty}^{y} F(y)dy \geq \int_{-\infty}^{y} G(y)dy$$

And. $\int_{-\infty}^{0} (F(y) - G(y))\, dy = 0$

$\Rightarrow F(\cdot)$ has more weight in lower outcome tail (left), even though means are equal.

This relates to concept of Stochastic Dominance —

Characterizes with in terms of cdf's compares mass, but allows for different means

Consider two cdf's — $F(y)$, $G(y)$

$G(y)$ is 2nd degree stochastically dominant over $F(y)$ if

$$\int_{-\infty}^{y} F(y)dy \geq \int_{-\infty}^{y} G(y)dy$$

Problems with Expected Utility Theory

Experimental and real — world data often illustrate "paradoxes" of EU theory —

1) "Certainty Effect" (Machina + Marschak) — an example of intransitive behavior that reflects a preference for certainty.
2) "Common Rates" (Khanneman Tversky) — another example of intransitive behavior.

3) Contextual Behaviour — "losses" may bear extra costs, status issues, crises effects.

Uncertainty in Production

— Yield risk
— Price risk (input and output)
— Liability
— Input reliability and availability (big in CA)
— Government policy uncertainty

Mechanisms Used to Manage Risk

— Futures markets
— Insurance (crop and options)
— Contracts
— Warranties

Sandmo's Model

Model of competitive firm facing price uncertainty (only),

$$\text{Firm max } EU(\Pi) = \max_{Y} EU(P \cdot Y - C(Y) + w_o)$$

w_0 = wealth stock

$$FONC - \frac{\partial L}{\partial Y} = EU'(P \cdot Y - C(Y) + w_0)(P - C'(Y)) = 0$$

we know —

$$E(XY) = E(X) \cdot E(Y) + \text{cov}(X, Y)$$

which implies *FONC* is —

$$(P - C'(Y)) + \frac{\text{Cor}(u'(w), P - C'(Y))}{EU'(w)} = 0$$

Where $w = p\ .\ y–C(Y) + w_0$
We know $w = p\ .\ y–C(y) + w_0$

$$E(w) = \overline{p} \cdot Y - C(Y) + w_0$$

So — take these two together —

$$w - E(w) = (p - \overline{p})Y$$
$$w = E(w) + (p - \overline{p})Y.$$

If $p > \overline{p}$, we know $w > E(w)$ and

$$u'(w) \leq u'(E(w))$$

multiply each side by $(p - \overline{p})$ —

$$(p - \overline{p})u'(w) \leq u'(E(w))(p - \overline{p})$$

take expectations of each side and note that $E(w)$ is a fixed number — you get —

$$E\left[u'(w)(p - \overline{p})\right] \leq u'(E(w)) \cdot E(p - \overline{p}).$$

But, we know $E(p - \overline{p}) = 0$, so —

$$E\left[u'(w)(p \cdot \overline{p})\right] \leq 0$$

we can rewrite this as —

$$E\left[u'(w)\right](C'(Y) - \overline{p}) \leq 0$$

which implies $C'(Y) \leq \overline{p}$

*Risk averse firms will produce less than risk neutral firms.

Consider again the FONC —

$$\frac{\partial L}{\partial Y} = Eu'(p \cdot y - C(Y) + w_0)\,(p - C'(Y)) = 0$$

SOC is —

$$\frac{\partial^2 L}{\partial Y^2} = EU''(p - C(Y))^2 - Eu'C''(Y) < 0$$

Total differentiation of FOC wrt w_0 yields —

$$\frac{dY}{dw_0} = -\frac{Eu''(p - C(y))}{\partial^2 L / \partial Y^2}.$$

If we have DARA, we know $-\frac{u''}{u'} < R_A(\tilde{w})$ with $p < \tilde{p}$ and $w > \tilde{w}$ ($\tilde{w}$ = wealth at $p = \tilde{p}$).

Thus, we know — for every w —

$$-\frac{u''}{u'}(p - C'(Y)) < R_A(\tilde{w})(p - C'(Y))$$

Which implies $-u''(p - C'(Y)) < R_A(\tilde{w})u'(p - C'(Y))$ we know RHS = 0 from FONC thus LHS of this must be less than zero.

This allows us to sign $\partial y/\partial w_0 \Rightarrow$

$$\frac{\partial Y}{\partial w_0} \begin{array}{c} > \\ = \\ < \end{array} 0 \quad \text{AS} \quad \frac{\partial R_A}{\partial w_0} \begin{array}{c} < \\ = \\ > \end{array} 0.$$

Mean-Variance Approach

Dates to Tobin + Markowitz

Idea is to describe utility that is dependent on random variables as a Taylor's series expansion —

$$E(u) = \int u(y) f(y)\, dy$$

$$u(y) = u(\bar{y}) + u'(\bar{y})(y - \bar{y}) + u''(\bar{y})\frac{(y - \bar{y})^2}{2} + \sum_{n=3}^{\infty} u^n \frac{(y - \bar{y})^n}{n!}$$

which, when we take expectations of both sides, yields —

$$Eu(y) = u(\bar{y}) + \sum_{n=z}^{\infty} \frac{u^n(\bar{y})}{n!} E(y - \bar{y})^n = f(m_1, \ldots, m_n)$$

$$\uparrow$$

function of moments

If function can be entirely defined by first n moments, *EU* is function of these first n moments.

If a distribution of a random variable can be defined by first 2 moments, then *EU* is function of mean and variance only.

Under certain restrictions on utility function and distribution of random variables —

— utility is quadratic or exponential

— outcome variable is normally distributed, we can write —

$$EU(y) = \alpha \bar{y} + \beta \frac{\sigma^2}{2}$$

Problems with this —

1) Quadratic utility implies IARA
2) Exponential utility implies CARA
3) Distribution of R.V. may not be normal —
   — e.g. crop yields negatively skewed (beta or gamma)
   — commodity prices positively skewed (ln normal)

A few quick points on meaning risk (to be covered in greater detail below) —

1) Econometric specification of Just and Pope (1977) —
   2 options for econometric models —
   Additive risk $y = f(x) + \varepsilon$ where $E(\varepsilon) = 0$
   Multiplicative risk $y = f(x) \,.\, \varepsilon$ where $E(\varepsilon) = 1$
   As we will see later, Just and Pope criticize both

- — additive specification does not allow uncertainty effect to be correlatted with input mix
- — multiplicative specification does not allow inputs to have different impacts on mean and variance (e.g — fertilizer = mean increasing but variance reducing)

Thus, they suggest

$$y = f_1(x) + f_2(x)\,\varepsilon \quad \text{with } E(\varepsilon) = 0$$

Problem is that this gets very complicated to apply.

2) Exponential Utility —

$$u\,(x) = 1 - e^{-\delta x}$$

$E\,(u(x) = m(-\delta)$ moment severity form
Shortcoming — implies CARA

3) Expo — power utility function

   Saha (1993) proposed more flexible exponential form —

   $u(w) = \theta - \exp(-\beta w^{\alpha})$ $\quad \theta > 1$

   $\alpha \neq 0$

   $\beta \neq 0$

   $\alpha\beta > 0$

Nice properties:

1) Unique up to affine transformation
2) $-\dfrac{u''}{u'} = \dfrac{1+\alpha\beta w^{\alpha}}{w}$ and $\dfrac{u''}{u'} w = 1+\alpha\beta w^{\alpha}$
3) For $\alpha < 1 \Rightarrow$ DARA

   $\alpha = 1 \Rightarrow$ CARA

   $\alpha > 1 \Rightarrow$ IARA
4) $\beta < 0 \Rightarrow$ DRRA, IARA
5) $u(\cdot)$ is quasi — concave for all $w > 0$

   Has realized guide a bit of practical use in dg econ.

The Ag Producer Under Uncertainty + Risk Aversion

(Moschini & Hennessy)

2 major sources of uncertainty —

— Production (inherent sources of uncertainty)

— Prices (not known when production decisions are made)

Consider price risk — choose g to max $E\left[u(w_0 + \tilde{\Pi})\right]$ where $\tilde{\Pi}$ is profit subject to price uncertainty and w_0 = initial wealth —

$$\tilde{\Pi} = \tilde{p}q - \underbrace{C(g,r)}_{\text{Variable cost form}} - \underbrace{k}_{\text{fixed cost}}$$

This is Sandmo's model (discussed above).

If production function is stochastic, a standard cost function is not valid and thus we must amend this to —

$$\tilde{\Pi} = p \cdot G(x,\tilde{e}) - rX - K$$

$G(x,\tilde{e})$ = stochastic production function for inputs X + random shock $\tilde{e}$.

Case of production uncertainty is harder to handle.

In reality, both sources of uncertainty matter and we must write problem with both sources.

Let's assume production risk is multiplicative — production function $= \tilde{e} \cdot H(x)$ with $E(\tilde{e}) = 1$

Problem becomes: $\tilde{\Pi} = \tilde{p}\tilde{e}H(x) - rX - K$

Many have noted that, in this case, there is a standard cost function that is conditional on expected output —

$$\breve{\Pi} = \tilde{p}\tilde{e}\bar{g}C(\bar{g},r) - K$$

Some implicit assumptions here:

— model is static
— one output
— no risk management strategies

Moschini and Hennessy present a simplified framework for considering various aspects of production under uncertainty —

Consider an expected profit maximizer facing a profile of profit opportunities $Z(\alpha,\beta,\tilde{\varepsilon})$ (Risk Neutral Case)

a = vector of actions

β = vector of exogenous parameters

$\tilde{\varepsilon}$ = single random variable that follows —

$cdf = F(\varepsilon)$

$\varepsilon \in [0,1]$

$$\text{Producer's problem is: } \max_{a} \int_0^1 Z(a,\beta,\varepsilon)\, dF(\varepsilon)$$

which yields FOC's — $\int_0^1 Z_a(a,\beta,\varepsilon)\, dF(\varepsilon) = 0$ where $Z_a = \partial z/\partial a$

One example — Sandmo's problem of pure price risk —

$$a = g$$
$$\tilde{p} = \beta_1 + (\tilde{\varepsilon} - \bar{\varepsilon})\beta_2 \quad \text{where } \bar{\varepsilon} = E(\tilde{\varepsilon})$$

$\beta_1 + \beta_2$ are location and scale parameters — mean price $= \bar{p} = \beta$
Variation of price represented by β_2

If production is also stochastic $\tilde{\varepsilon}$ cannot be separated out so easily. Results not so clear —

In such case, increasing $\tilde{\varepsilon}$ does not necessarily increase a.

Now consider risk averse case —

$$\text{Payoff} = Z(a, \beta, \tilde{\varepsilon})$$

$$\text{Objective} \quad \max_a \int_0^1 u(z(a, \beta, \varepsilon)\, dF(\varepsilon)$$

$$FOC - \int_0^1 U_z\left[Z(a,\beta,\varepsilon)\right] \cdot Z_a(a,\beta,\varepsilon)\, dF(\varepsilon) = 0 \text{ solution} = \text{a*}$$

With uncertainty, this implies (FOC) $\Rightarrow$

$$\text{Cov}[u_Z(\cdot), Z_a(\cdot)] + E(u_Z(\cdot)) \cdot E(_{Za}(\cdot)) = 0$$

If $Z_{a\varepsilon} \geq 0$ implies (along with risk aversion)

$$\text{Cov}\ [u_Z(\cdot), Z_a(\cdot)] \leq 0$$

And $E(Z_a(\cdot)) \geq 0$.

Now consider marginal changes in the environment — e.g., increase in expected price $\Rightarrow \Delta\beta > 0$

Differentiate FOC w.r.t $a + \beta$ —

$$\frac{da^*}{d\beta} = \frac{1}{\Delta}\int_0^1 A[z]z_\beta(\cdot)u_z(\cdot)Z_a(\cdot)\, dF(\varepsilon)$$
$$-\frac{1}{\Delta}\int_0^1 u_z(\cdot)z_{a\beta}(\cdot)\, dF(\varepsilon)$$

Where A[·] = – u_{zz}/u_z = coefficient ARA.
Where Δ = *SOC* (assumed to be < 0)

Note $\Delta = \int_0^1 u_{zz}(\cdot)(z_x(\cdot))^2 + u_z(\cdot)z_{aa}\, dF(\varepsilon) < 0$

Hennessey (1998) partitions this overall effect into 3 parts

(A) = wealth effect
(B) = insurance effect
(C) = coupling effect

Consider coupling effect:

$$(c) = -\int_0^1 u_z(\cdot)z_{ab}(\cdot)\, dF(\varepsilon)/\Delta \Rightarrow \text{ Has sign of } z_{ab}$$

So, if β increases marginal effect of *a* on payoff Z(·) — increase in β will increase more use of *a*.

Note, "decoupled" program implies $Z_{ab} = 0$

Moschini and Hennessey show wealth effects depend on risk preferences (as would be expected) + $\Delta\beta \Rightarrow$ increase *a*

Insurance effect — if $Z\beta c(\cdot) \leq 0$ (Exogenous shift stabilizes income) then $\Delta a > 0$

What about duality results? Does cost min continue to hold? Yes, rules certain restrictions —

Consider competitive firm choosing *X* to max —

$$E(u(w_0 + \tilde{\Pi}))$$

where $\tilde{\Pi} = R(x, \tilde{\varepsilon}) - rx$ R(·)=revenue
Pope and Chavas have shown, if revenue satisfies —

$$R(x, \tilde{\varepsilon}) = K(\Psi(x), \tilde{\varepsilon})$$

Then a relevant cost function can be written as —

$C(g^{\Psi},r)$ where g^{Ψ} is vector of conditioning values corresponding to $\Psi(x)$

Simple case — multiplicative risk —

$$R(x,\tilde{\varepsilon}) = H(x) \cdot \tilde{\varepsilon}$$

As we have shown, this yields cost function $C(\overline{g},r)$

Where $\overline{g}$ = expected output.

Contingent Markets and Insurance

Let's simplify all of this to consider case of 2 states of nature —

Loss — P(loss) = Π

No loss — p(No loss) = $1 - \Pi$

w = wealth

u = utility function

L = loss amount

This implies that endorsement of economy is

$$(w - L)\,\Pi + w(1 - \Pi)$$

Consider an insurance contract —

— Collects premium = α

— L_0 paid L if a loss occurs

Actuarially fair insurance premium = Expected loss

$$\alpha = \Pi \cdot L$$

Income of insuring agent —

$w - \alpha = w - \Pi\, L$ if he does not have accident

$w - L + L - \alpha = w - \Pi\, L$ if he does have an accident

In other words, equal — putting him on fair odds

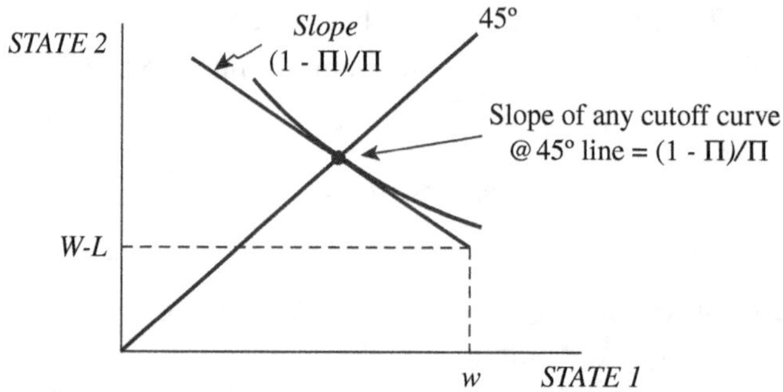

* In a risk averse agent (any degree of risk aversion) a fundamental fact — at a premium of $\alpha = \Pi L$, insurance will be complete.

Let agent select insurance coverage (Z) and let's charge agent g per unit of compensation in case of an accident.

Actuarial fairness $\Rightarrow g = \Pi$

Consumer problem =

$$\underset{x_1, x_2, Z}{\text{Max}}\ (1 - \Pi)\, u(x_1) + \Pi u(x_2)$$

$$\text{s.t. } x_1 = w - gz \qquad \leftarrow \text{No loss}$$
$$x_2 = w - L + z - gz \qquad \leftarrow \text{Loss}$$

$$\Rightarrow \underset{x_1, x_2, z}{\text{Max}}\ [(1 - \Pi)\, u(w - gz) + (\Pi) u(w - L + z - gz)]$$

FONC — $(1 - \Pi)\, z\, u^1\, (w - gz) = \Pi\, (1 - g)\, u'\, (w - L + z - gz)$
If $g = \Pi$, this implies —

$$u'\,(w - gz) = u'\,(w - L + z - gz)$$
$$\text{OR} \Rightarrow 3 = L \text{ (complete ins.!)}$$

Moral Hazard

Assume now that the probability of loss is endogenous to an agent's actions.

Agent can influence probability by exercising self protection = x
$\Pi(x)$ = function describing how X influences Π

Agent's Problem

$w - x - \Pi(x)\, z$	if no loss
$w - x - L - \Pi(x)\, z + 3$	if loss occurs

Consumer solves following :

$$\underset{X\,z}{\text{Max}}\ [\Pi(x)\, u(w - L - x + (1 - \Pi(x))\, z) + (1 - \Pi(x)\, \text{u}\, (w - x - \Pi(x)\, z)]$$

$FOC \rightarrow$ Define (2) = loss state
(1) = no loss state

(1) $[u(2) - u(1)]\, \Pi'(x) - \Pi(x)\, (1 + \Pi'(x)\, \delta)\, u'(2)$
$- (1 - \Pi(x))\, (1 + \Pi'(x)\, \delta)\, u'(1) = 0$

(2) $\Pi(x)\, [1 - \Pi(x)]\, u'(2) - [1 - \Pi(x)]\, \Pi(x)\, u'(1) = 0$
(2) implies $u'(2) = u'(1)$ = insurance is complete (δ = L)
This simplifies (2) to $1 + \Pi'(x)\, L = 0$
Problem occurs if company sets a price independent of observing x.
Optimization Problem Becomes —

$$\underset{\delta,\, x}{Max}\ \left[\Pi(x)u(w - x - L + \delta\,(1 - g)) + (1 - \Pi(x))u(w - x - \delta\, g)\right]$$

*Note g = price of insurance $\Rightarrow$ not affected by x

(3) This implies: $\Pi'(x)\, [u(2) - u(1)\,] - \Pi(x)\, u'(1) - (1 - \Pi(x)\, u'(2) \leq 0 =$ 0 if $x > 0$

(4) And $\Pi(x)\, (1 - g)\, u'(2) - (1 - \Pi(x))\, g\, u'(1) = 0$
Zero profits requires $g^* = \Pi(x^*)$
Where x^* = optional level of self protection
(4) implies $u'(2) = u'(1) \Rightarrow$ complete insurance
(3) implies — $u^1\,(1) < 0$

$$= 0 \text{ if } x^* > 0$$

Since $u'(1) > 0$ must hold, we know $x^* = 0$

$X^* = 0 \Rightarrow$ In competitive equilibrium, agents will exercise zero self protection if rates do not reflect their level of self protection

This is basic case of moral hazard

Note, another competitive equilibrium exists in which price of insurance leads agents to use x to totally self insure

$$\Pi(x)\, u(w - x - L) + (1 - \Pi(x))\, u(w - x)$$

So — complete moral hazard can result in a failure of insurance markets.

A way that insurance can improve on this problem is by using coinsurance —

Adverse selection and pooling equilibrium — (from Rothschild and Stiglitz 1977) —

Problem is that risks are heterogeneous in potential pool of insurance buyers — and insurer cannot observe the risks —

2 Agents with same utility function

But agents differ in risk of loss, which they can observe, but insurer cannot

Insurer can only observe aggregate risk — and they set a common price g

Agents' risk — Π_H = high risk agent

Π_L = less risk agent

g = common price of insurance

High risk agent's problem —

$$\underset{Z}{Max}\left[\Pi_H u(w - L - gZ + Z) + (1 - \Pi_H) u(w - gZ)\right]$$

Which yields $\dfrac{u'(w - L - gZ + Z)}{u'(w - gZ)} = \dfrac{(1 - \Pi_H)g}{\Pi_H(1 - g)} g$

Likewise for low risk agent

$$\frac{u'(w-L-gZ+Z)}{u'(w-gZ)} = \frac{(1-\Pi_L)g}{\Pi_L(1-g)}$$

Since $\Pi_H > \Pi_L$, we know —

$$\frac{(1-\Pi_L)}{\Pi_L} > \frac{(1-\Pi_H)}{\Pi_H}$$

Which requires $Z_H > Z_L$!
Basic result — high risk agent overinsures low risk agent underinsures
This is classic case of adverse selection —

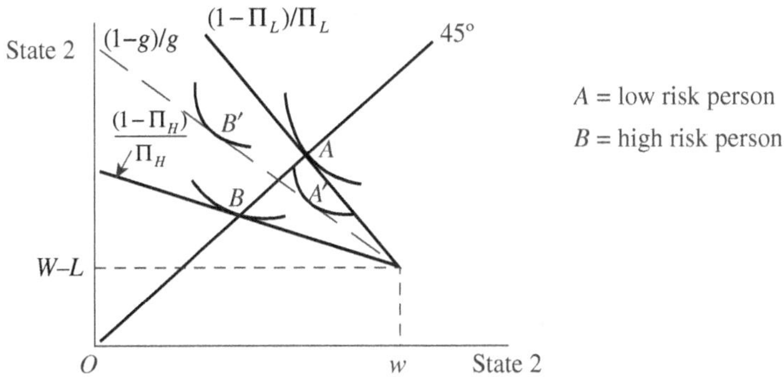

If risks were priced accurately, agents A and B would fully insure at A and B.

However, at a common price of g —

— Agent A underinsures (falls short of 45°)
— Agent B overinsures (left of 45°)

A problem of adverse selection can occur as the risk of the insurance pool can be shifted to higher risk individuals.

Death Spiral of Adverse Selection —

— Adverse selection leads to overinsurance by higher risk, underinsurance by low risks
— Insurance plan loses money
— Insurer attempts to compensate by raising premium g
— But, this serves to only worsen the problem as lower risks are driven out of the pool
— Insurance pool becomes
  — smaller
  — riskier
— Eventually collapses — a real world problem!

This is the same equilibrium as that described by Akerlof's (1970) market for lemons — only defective case (high risks) are left in the market.

Rothschild and Stiglitz talk about types of equilibrium that insurance markets can reach —

— Pooling contracts
— Separating contracts (only thing viable)

Separating contracts depend on being able to identify and respond to agents by risks.

Insurance markets very effective at achieving this, although adverse selection remains a big problem in crop insurance.

Chapter 6

Crop Insurance

A major research area — very important topic in agecon + policy.

I have asked you to read 3 of my papers on the topic —

A Brief Overview

1) Goodwin 1993 — "Empirical Analysis of Demand for Crop Insurance"
   Background for paper was an argument by GAO that premium rates were too low, and hence this was why program was losing money.
   An alternative explanation ⇒ Adverse selection
   Recall that adverse selection arises due to inaccurate premium rates.
   Trick of this paper was to allow producers response to premium changes to vary with risk — measured by loss rates.
   Application is to country level corn data.
   Paper finds that elasticity of demand (response of insurance demand to premium changes) depends on risk (adverse selection)
   Higher risk ⇒ less elastic demand.
   Implication — raising all premium rates (across the board) may actually worsen performance of program as low risk individuals are driven out.
2) 1994 Paper on Premium Rates + Risk →
   Paper discusses methods used to measure risk (+ estimate premium rates) in the federal program.
   A few points —
   RMA essentially assumes that higher average yield implies more risk.

However, may not always hold →

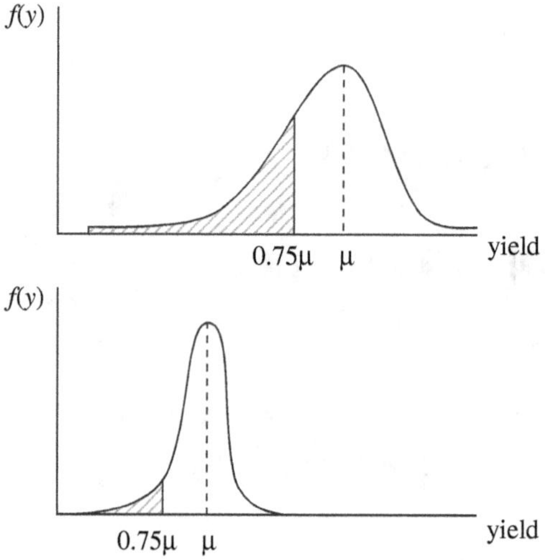

Highest yield actually has more risk

Look at factors related to yield Expected Value. There is a tendency for their relationship to hold — but much variation across farms (see case of low R^2 in regressions)

Note — FCIC/RMA no longer uses normal curve theory to rate contracts.

Instead an empirical type of rate is used.

Brief discussion — what is the actuarially — fair insurance premium rate?

Key question for a great deal of research

Actuarially fair means ⇒

Expected premium = expected losses

Definitions:

Insurance Premium Rate = \$ paid per \$100 of coverage
= % of liability paid as premium
= E (Loss)/Liability

Liability = maximum total loss

Premium = Total \$ paid for coverage
= Rate * Liability

Indemnity = A loss payment

Suppose the object of coverage, y, is a random variable with pdf = $f(y)$

E (Loss) is amount that insurers should collect in an actuarially fair contract.

A convenient way to write it is as:

$$\text{Prob (Loss)} \cdot \text{E (Loss|Loss occurs)}$$

Suppose one contract will insure some proportion of the mean $\lambda \cdot \mu$.

If y is less than $\lambda\mu$, the insurers will pay ($\lambda\mu$–y) as an indemnity

So, payouts = max (0, $\lambda\mu$–y)

For one distribution f(y) – prob(loss) = prob(y < $\lambda\mu$)

$$\text{prob}(\text{loss}) = \int_{-\infty}^{\lambda\mu} f(y)dy$$

$$\text{E(loss|loss occurs)} = \lambda\mu - \left[\int_{-\infty}^{\lambda u} y.f(y)dy \bigg/ \int_{-\infty}^{\lambda u} f(y)dy \right]$$

Note importance of proper specification of $f(y)$

So, put these together —

$$E(\text{Loss}) = \int_{-\infty}^{\lambda u} f(y)dy \cdot \left[\lambda u - \frac{\int_{-\infty}^{\lambda u} yf(y)\,dy}{\int_{-\infty}^{\lambda u} f(y)\,dy} \right]$$

To put then in rate terms

$$\text{Rate} = \text{E(loss)}/\lambda\mu$$

3) Paper on problems with market insurance —

Some facts about crop insurance in U.S. —

- — In existence since 1938 (as federal program)
- — Specific peril coverage in existence since 1797 (typically covers hail, fire, etc.)
- — MPCI = "multiple peril crop insurance"

— Current programs driven by 1980 Act
— Significantly expanded by 1994 CIRA and 2000 ARPA
— Total liability exceeds ≈$ 145 billion
— Heavily subsidized
  — Premiums 50–60 %
  — Subsidies paid to private companies to market and service insurance
  — SRA = Standard Reinsurance Agreement
  — Govt. is reinsurer
  — SRA allows companies to "assign risk" to a pool (shift fail policies to the government)
  — SRA also limits how much a company can lose in bad years
— If an actuarially fair premium is given 50% subsidy, insurance buyer receives $2 back for each $1 paid in premium
— For US, between 1981-2005, each $1 is premium paid yielded $2.05 is indemnities (this is producer — paid premium)
— Premium subsidies paid as % of premium — which implies more risk ⇒ more subsidy
— Raises question ⇒ does the program encourage more risk in agriculture?
— Ad hoc disaster relief also an issue — $26 billion given between 1986–2005 (free insurance?)
— Is this disincentive to buy and does it further skew participation toward high risks?
— Systemic risk
  — Often used to argue for why government must be involved
  — Basically reflects weather pattern
  — See discussion in paper
  — Maybe correlation is state-dependent
  — Means catastrophic losses could be extreme (value of US corn crop in a typical year = $100 + billion)
— Area risk and index — insurances
  — U.S. has GRP + GRIP plans
— Revenue risk – income (p^*t) = TR ⇒
  — takes advantage of the "natural hedge"
  — adds new critical parameter = correlation coefficient

Modeling Yields

Typically considered for purposes of rating crop insurance.
Key issues ⇒

1) Remove deterministic effects (time trends, structural breaks, etc.)
2) Farm level (rare) vs. aggregate (e.g. county)
3) Systemic risks, pooling, etc.
4) Parametric vs non-parametric

How to remove deterministic factors —

Standard approach — detrended regression —

$$y_t = \alpha + \beta_1 t + \beta_2 t^2 + e_t$$

we commonly "recenter" on last prediction

$\hat{y}_T$ = predicted volume for last observation (or sometimes for out of sample prediction)

$\hat{y}_t^T$ = value for time t, scaled to be comparable to $\hat{y}_T$

$$\hat{y}_t^T = \hat{y}_T^T + e_t$$

Another approach considers residuals (departures from trend) in proportional terms — under idea that bigger means should imply bigger errors deviations.

$$\hat{u}_t = \frac{\hat{e}_t}{\hat{Y}_t}$$

$$\hat{y}_t^T = (1 + \hat{u}_t)\hat{y}_T^T$$

Note an issue here — we are using a first stage estimation to detrend and then treating the resulting detrended data as if it were observed without error.

This will understate variance of yields and thus rates.

A better approach would be to estimate trends and rates together — something we have done in a recent paper.

Parametric Approach

CLT tells us that any mean of iid data (regardless of distribution) converge to a normal distribution.

So why not use normality?

Experience tells us that average yields, even for the county-level, tend to be negatively skewed.

Problem with CLT is iid assumption — spatial correlation violates this.

3 common parametric approaches —

1) Normality (widely debated article by Just and Weninger 1999 AJAE– argued in favor of normality).
   Many early crop insurance rating methods assumed normality.
   However, evidence strong against normality (Just and Weninger had too small samples).
2) Beta — very common!
   Remember — Beta defined over [0,1] interval.
   For this standard beta shape defined by two parameters (α,β)
   We also sometimes work with 4-parameter Beta-where data are scaled by $[\sigma\text{-}\theta]$ to lie between min possible = θ and max possible (σ).
   θ,σ hard to estimate and often are fixed by assumption (though note that the distribution may be very sensitive to this)
   Common Beta Shape:

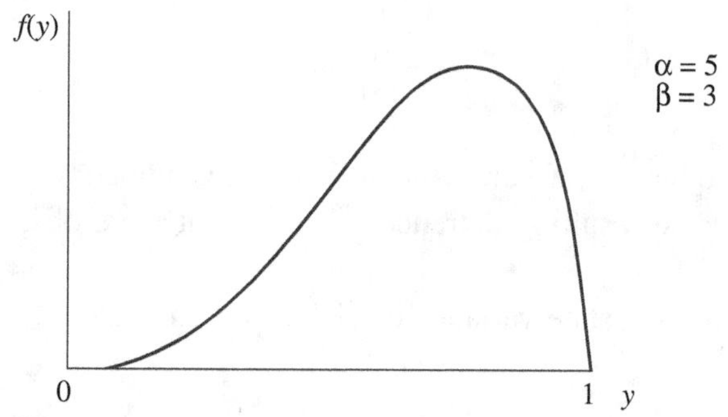

3) Mixtures —

$$f(y) = \lambda\varphi_1(y) + (1-\lambda)\ \varphi_2(y)$$

Where $\varphi_i(\cdot)$ = a pdf component
λ = mixing parameter ($0 \le \lambda \le 1$)

Note — allows nested-type testing, though it is complicated by fact that parameters of φ_1 unidentified under H_0: $\lambda = 0$ and vice versa for φ_2 with H_0: $\lambda = 1$.

This type of density relatively common for crops where tail represents a "catastrophic" event.

Example — Mixture of Normals

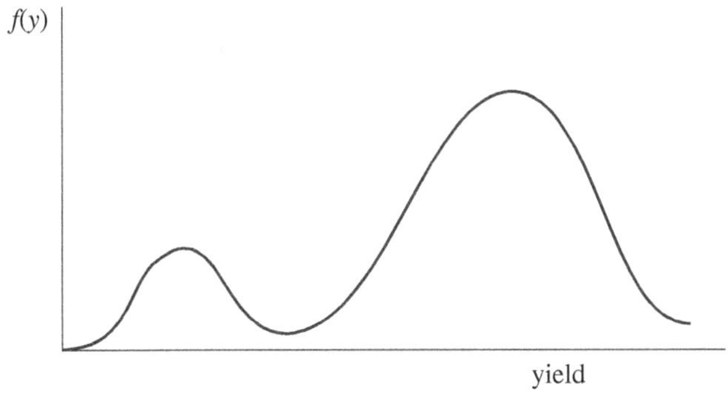

A number of other densities are used to model crop yields — weibull, beta, gamma, etc.

Nonparametric Distributions

Remember the age — old tradeoff often repeated in statistics and econometrics —

More structure ⇒ — if correct = more efficiency
— if incorrect = bias

So — imposing more structure (e.g., a specific parametric family) involves a bias-efficiency tradeoff.

If I know the structure, inefficient to not impose it.

If I am wrong and impose it — end up with bias.

Semi-parametric and non-parametric distribution impose less structure on the problem.

Suitability of non-parametric procedures often depends on sample size — need relatively large samples to start relaxing structure

Simplest nonparametric approach —

Empirical Distributions —

Simplest case = histogram (we all have used).

*Empirical estimates frequently used to rate crop insurance (US program uses this).

Problem, need a lot of data —

example — corn yield —

Suppose average yield = 100 bu and you want to consider a contract that will pay for any shortfall beneath 75 bu (enough to buy you back to 75 bu), you look back in data and consider average level of payouts had this plan been in place —

e.g.	yield	indemnity
	80	0
	60	15
	100	0
	120	0
	40	35
	55	20
	.	.
	.	.
	.	.

Average indemnity = E(Loss)

$$\text{Rate}=\frac{E(\text{Loss})}{\text{Liability}}=\frac{\text{Average Indemnity}}{75}$$

This is probably used more often then anything else in actual rating exercises.

Digression — rating by simulation —

We can do anything very similar when working with parametric distributions.

In this case — 2 approaches to integration —

1) Analytical Integration — work with analytical solutions
2) Integration by Monte Carlo — simulate large number of realizations from your parametric distributions. (usually much easier).

Example — suppose yields ~ Beta ($\alpha = 5$, $\beta = 3$)

Generate 10,000 yields from Beta ($\cdot$) and calculate empirical rates for them — if # of simulation large enough — gives same answer as analytical

Some side notes on using SAS to simulate parametric distributions and crop insurance parameters —

A model fact — cdf value for any distribution is distributed as uniform — so we can simulate by generating random uniform variates on [0,1] interval, plug them into inverse cdf function (SAS uses the "quantile" function) and thus generate from any distribution.

Mechanics of measuring insurance parameters if you have simulated yield series($y_1,\ldots,y_T$)

Say you generate from Beta (7,4) on [0,225]

Insurance guarantee is 125 bu. — so any yield $y_t < 125$ gets a payment $(125\text{-}y_t)$.

Assume each unit is paid at a price = 1 (rates are transparent to this).

Coding

Loss = max $(0,125 - y_t)$, Average = E(Loss)

Probability of Loss —

$$P = (y_t < 125); \quad \leftarrow = 1 \text{ if } y_t < 125 \qquad 0 \quad \textit{otherwise}$$

Take average of this over replications — gives estimate of probability of loss.

E(y|y < 125) →

$$= \int_0^{125} y \cdot f(y)\, dy \Big/ \int_0^{125} f(y)\, dy$$

if y < 125 then d = y ; $\underbrace{\text{else d=}\cdot\text{;}}_{\text{optional}}$

Take the average — yields $E(y|y < 125)$.

Rate = E(Loss)/125 —

Note here why price does not matter — cancels on top and bottom.

I find it very useful to work in this way as I can better envision the mechanics of the distribution.

Nonparametric Methods

Several approaches — nearest neighbors, histograms, etc.

Most common — Kernel Density Estimates —

Read Goodwin and Ker (1998) for application to crop insurance —

The idea — we choose a function with a desirable shape — a "kernel"

Examples —

Epanechnikov —

Triangular

Normal

Define K(·) = Kernel

Must satisfy $\int_{-\infty}^{\infty} K(t)dt = 1$

The "width" of a kernel is determined by a parameter called the "bandwidth"

For a normal kernel, you can think of bandwidth as a variance – measure.

The mechanics of nonparametric kernel density estimation involves "surrounding" each observation by a function and "adding up" area under functions —

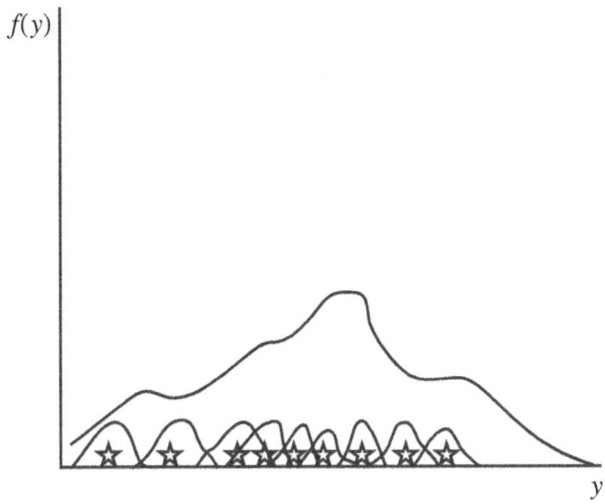

Note — wider the bandwidth, the smoother is the function

Kernel estimate of a density is given by —

$$\hat{f}(x) = \frac{1}{nh}\sum_i K\left(\frac{X - X_i}{h}\right). \qquad h = \text{bandwidth}$$

Goodwin + Ker 1998 AJAE —

Used these methods to rate area-wide crop insurance plans.

Note an a inconsistency in using $y = x\beta$ to detrend

— OLS sort of assumes symmetric error distribution (OLS is nonparametric — but can make errors "more symmetric")
— Argument made in form of OLS in quadratic loss setting
Note figure # 2, 3 — resulting densities

One problem — assumption of a constant bandwidth parameter — if data are "trended" — tends to under smooth in regions where data are thin + vice versa

Also — discussion of pooling across centers and non-independence issues (use weighting)

Ker + Goodwin — later AJAE paper — revisit the problem using hierarchical Bayesian methods to improve estimates

Supplemented Notes on Nonparametric Regression

A simple extension of nonparametric density estimation —

$$E(y|x) = m(x) \qquad\qquad m(\cdot) = \text{unknown function}$$

So, we have — $y = m(x) + \varepsilon$ and $E(\varepsilon|x) = 0$
Standard OLS $\Rightarrow m(x) = a + \beta\cdot x$
Several ways of lifting the parametric restrictions.
We will discuss a few —

1) Nadaraya — Watson estimation — direct analog to kernel density
— Often call this kernel regression —

$$\text{We know } E(y\,|\,x) = \int_{-\infty}^{\infty} y\, f(y|x)\, dy$$

In a manner analogous to what was done to estimate density —

$$\hat{m}(x) = \frac{\sum_{i=1}^{n} K\left(\frac{X - X_i}{h}\right) \cdot y_i}{\sum_{i=1}^{n} K\left(\frac{X - X_i}{h}\right)}$$

Another way to look at it —

$$\hat{m}(x) = \sum_{i=1}^{n} w_i(x) \cdot y_i$$

$$\text{Where } w_i = \text{weight} = \frac{k\left((X - X_i)/h\right)}{\sum K\left(\frac{X - X_i}{h}\right)}$$

Weight represent distance that all X's are from individual X_i

Nadaraya — Watson estimates has some biases —

— arising from unequal spacing of observations

— noise at ends of data spread.

2) Local linear or nonlinear regression —

— estimate linear or polynomial OLS using values "close" to y_i, x_i

The local linear regression at point x corresponds to $\hat{\alpha}$ from —

$$\min_{\alpha,\, \beta} \sum K\left(\frac{x_i - x^0}{h}\right)\left[y_i - \alpha - \beta x_i\right]^2 \qquad \text{–so } \hat{m}(x^0) = \hat{\alpha} + \hat{\beta} X^0$$

⇒ a weighted least squares regression

Note NW regression is equivalent to this with $\beta = 0$

Locally weighted regression called "Lowess" or "Loess"

In SAS, we have

```
PROC LOESS;
MODEL y = x  /DEGREE = 1 or 2
              SELECT = GCV
              DIRECT;        (fit every point)
```

Computationally intensive.

3) Splines —

Splines are piecewise polynomials joined to make a single curve.
Simplest version — piecewise constant model
Partition X into $K + 1$ intervals (K = "Knot" point)

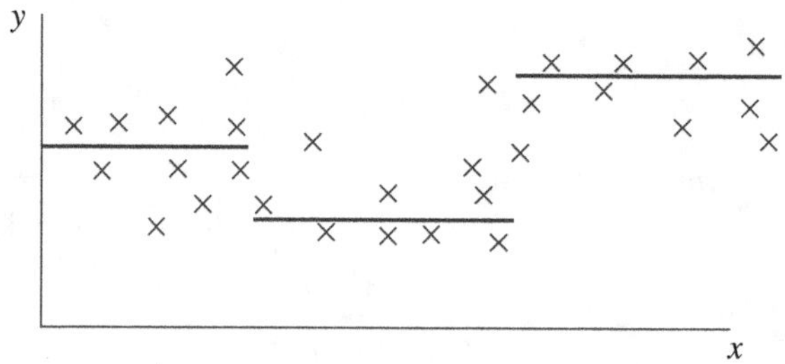

← 2 knots

$h_1(x) = \mathrm{I}(x<\varepsilon_1)$

$h_2(x) = \mathrm{I}(\varepsilon_1 \leq x<\varepsilon_2)$

$h_3(x) = \mathrm{I}(\varepsilon_2 \leq x)$

"Basic Functions"

Or, we could fit piecewise linear models —

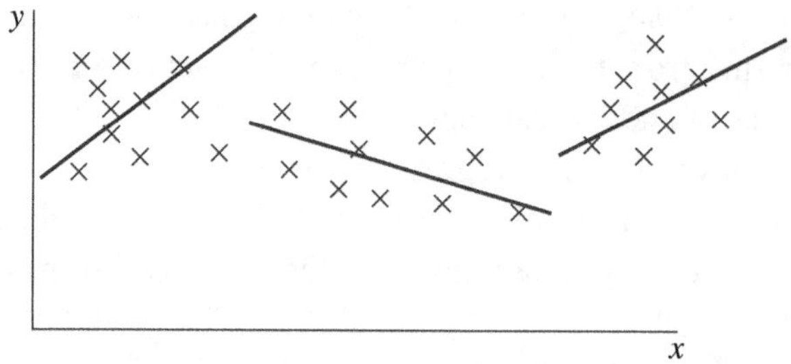

But these are not continuous — a better alternative —

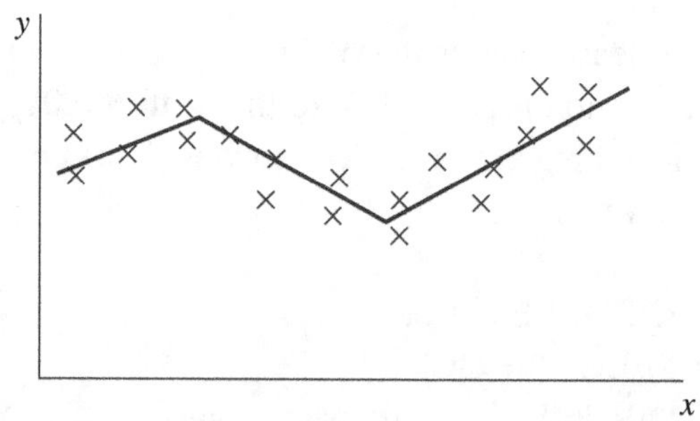

We do this by imposing constraints on basis functions —

$h_1(x) = 1$
$h_2(x) = x$
$h_3(x) = (x-\varepsilon_1)^+$
$h_4(x) = (x-\varepsilon_2)^+$

when $(\cdot)$ + denote positive portion of argument

$$r^+ = \begin{cases} r \text{ if } r \geq 0 \\ 0 \text{ if } r < 0 \end{cases}$$

So — with this we get a composite function $m(x)$ that is:
— everywhere continuous
— everywhere linear except at knots
— different slope for each region

we can ensure a function with continuous derivatives by using polynomials
— we typically use cubic splines.

In SAS — Several Procedures

PROC TPSPLINE
modes y = (x) /...

This plate spline — analogous to bending a sheet of metal — maintains continuity

Correlation, Association, and Copulas

As we have seen — the risk of a portfolio of assets may differ from that of individual assets —

It is lower if correlation is not perfect.
e.g. — risk on farm (as a whole) is less than risk on individual fields.
Recall — 2 random variables are independent if —

$$Prob_r(X \in A, y \in B) = Prob_{r}.(X \in A) \cdot Prob_r(y \in B)$$

Or, equivalently —

$$E\,(f(x)\cdot g(y)) = E\,(f(x))\cdot E(g(y))$$

for any functions $f(\cdot)$ and $g(\cdot)$

How do we typically measure this association?

⇒ correlation

Note however — although independent variables are uncorrelated, the converse does not necessary have to be true.

Independence ⇒ corr = 0 but corr = 0 ⇏ Independence.

Examples of uncorrelated but dependent variables:

— $X \sim N(0,1)$, $y = x^2$

— (x, y) uniformly distributed over circle of radius =1, centered on 0,0.

— (x, y) ~ t with zero correlation

— let $X_1, \ldots, X_n$ be iid random variables

N = counting distribution —

Then A = $x_1 + x_2 + \ldots + x_M$ and N are uncorrelated but not independent.

How do we typically measure correlation —

1) Pearson (linear) correlation —

$$\rho(x,y) = \frac{\operatorname{cov}(x,y)}{\sigma_x \cdot \sigma_y}$$

Note — $\rho = 1$ is implied for any a, and b > 0

$y = a + bx$ ($\rho = -1$ for b < 0)

2) Rank correlation (usually with Spearman correlation coefficient)

Consider set of random variables X_i —

If we order the observation low to high —

$$X_{(1)} < X_{(2)} < \ldots . < X_{(n)}$$

We say i is rank of $X(i)$

Spearman rank correlation is the correlation of the ranks

*Rank correlation is nonparametric because it is unvariant under monotonic transformations

e.g. — ρ_s for (x, y) same as —

— ρ_s for $(\ln(x), \ln(y))$ or

— ρ_s for $(\exp(x), \exp(y))$

For any continuous random variables (serial cdf is uniform distributed)

$$\rho_s = 12 \cdot E\,(F_x(x) - 0{\cdot}5)\,(F_y(y) - 0{\cdot}5)$$

Where $F(\cdot)$ is cdf

3.) Kendall's Tau —

Consider concordances and disconcordances between pairs of observation $(X_i - X_j, Y_i - Y_j)$ for $i + j$

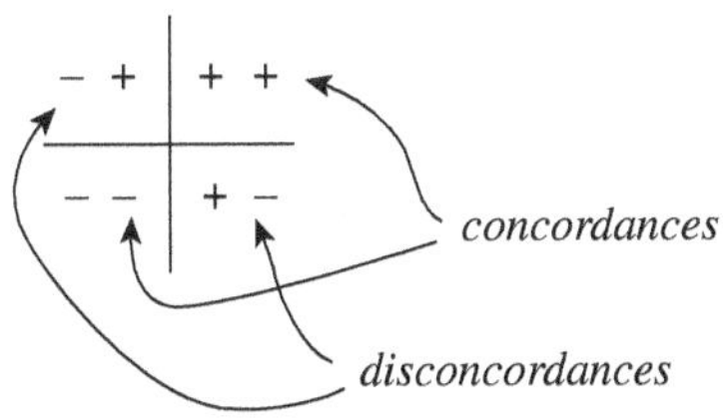

Remember that F(y) is ~ u (0,1)

for any cdf F(.)

This can be useful in transforming variables across different distributions while maintaining <u>rank</u> correlation

$$\text{e.g.} - \left.\begin{matrix} y_1 \sim F(y_1 \cdot) \\ X_1 \sim G(x_1) \end{matrix}\right\} \begin{matrix} F(\cdot) \\ G(\cdot) \end{matrix} \text{some unspecified continuous cdf}$$

If x_1, y_1 have rank correlation $\overline{\rho}_s$

For $\Phi(\cdot)$ = normal cdf —

Then $y_2 = \Phi^{-1}(F(y \cdot))$

$x_2 = \Phi^{-1}(G(x_1))$

Y_2, X_2 will have same rank correlation $\bar{p}_s$ but will be normally distributed.

Note — this is called using a "normal copula"

Copulas

A copula is a multivariate distribution whose marginals are uniform over (0, 1)

For any u = P dimensional vector on unit cube —

$$C(u_1, \ldots, u_p) = \text{Prob}(U_1 \leq u_1, \ldots, U_p \leq u_p)$$
$$C(\cdot) = \text{a "copula"}$$

Sklar's Theorem

If H(x) and G(y) are marginal cdf's for x + y, then the bivariate distribution of x, y can be defined as —

$$F(x, y) = C(H(x), C(y))$$

Where C(·) is a copula function.

Sklar's theorem implies C(·) always exists.

Consider what information is contained in C(·) that is not in the marginals —

- — Correlation (or dependence)
- — Relationships among higher ordered moments + cross – moments.

There is a wide range of different types of copulas that imply different types of relationships among random variables —

One example — non-constant (or state-dependent) linear correlation.

Examples —

Examples-

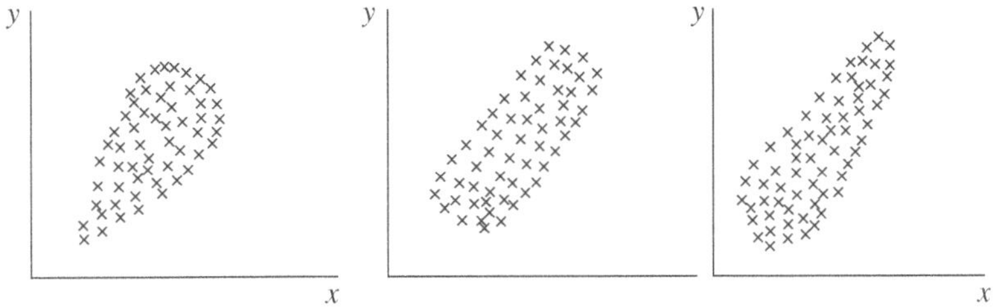

Clayton Frank Gumbel

And the most commonly used-

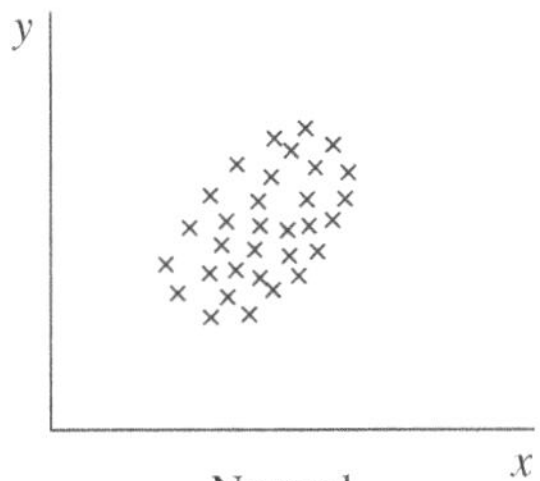

Normal

These parametric copulas are commonly characterized by a few parameters that describe the relationships.

How Do We Use Copulas?

1) Assume you know the family and estimate the relevant parameters (maybe theory tells you)
2) Estimate for several different copulas and compare goodness of fit (e.g., LLF, AIC, etc.)
   (Area of very active research)

Note — much of what is of interest in common problems is tail behavior — e.g. in insurance applications

You may not be able to adequately describe tail behavior with a copula unless you have large # observations.

Estimation of Copulas

2 Basic Approach

1) 2-step (called Inference Functions for Margins IFM)
   1) Estimate parameters of marginals (e.g., α,β for Beta)
   2) Then, holding them constant, estimate copula
   2A) Iterate if necessary.
2) Estimate everything at once using M.L.E.

In practice, these approaches typically yield similar results, though #2 is more efficient (and more difficult).

Another approach to modeling dependence —

The Iman-Conover method —

This is a simple method that "reorders" data to achieve a given desired rank-order correlation.

If normal scores are used in the method — it is equivalent to using a normal copula.

The I.C. Procedure

Consider an $n \times r$ matrix X (n observation $\times$ r marginals).

S = desired rank correlation matrix.

1) make column of scores for first column of X

$$a_i = \Phi^{-1}\left(\frac{1}{(n+1)} \right) \text{ for } i = 1, \dots, n$$

And rescale to have s.d. = 1 (divide by σ).

Note here — which Φ you use greatly impacts the resulting joint distribution

2) Randomize column of scores r times — and make new n × r matrix of resulting scores

$$M = a \,\|\, \tilde{a} \,\|\, \tilde{a} \ldots \|\, \tilde{a};$$

$\tilde{a}$ = random shuffle of scores.

3) compute correlation matrix S of M
4) Take Choleski decomposition of desired correlation S
   S = C′ C
5) compute $T = MF^{-1}\,C$
6) re-order original matrix X to have same rank ordering as T.
   This generates correlation structure as desired

Note though-using different score functions can change nature of correlation (same as different copulas)

Price + Revenue Risks

Many of the same issues arise for commodity prices.

A near-universal assumption for commodity prices ⇒ log normality (Black Scholes option pricing models assume)

In reality — seems to be an accurate choice, though in tails — behavior often refutes log normality —

It is common to work with "implied volatility" using options prices —

$$c(p_t) = \text{option price} = e^{rt} \int_0^{\infty} f(p_t) \max(0, p_T - S)\, d\, P_T$$

where p_t = commodity price
f (·) = price pdf
S = strike price

If I know the price, I can invert this and solve for distribution parameters (volatility)

One problem — you should get same parameters at any strike if you have correctly specified f (·) — but we often see difference —

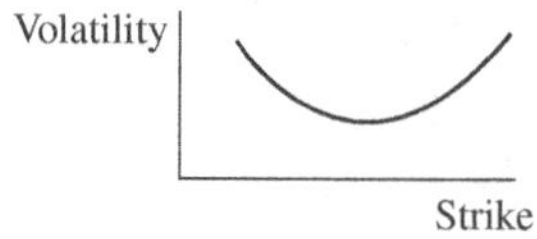

"Smile"

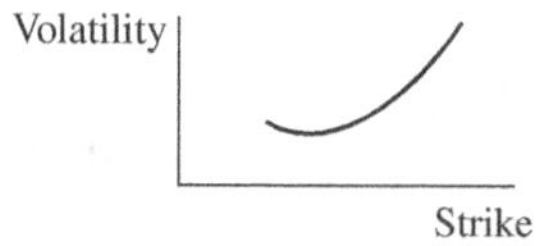

"Smirk"

So — evidence may not always support log normality

Modeling Revenue Risk —

We spoke about the fact that there are now many crop insurance plans that insure revenue = P·Q rather then just yield

So — we need to consider —

E (P)

E (Q)

Cov (P, Q) ← or ρ_{PQ} (typically < 0)

A neat and handy result — Rank correlation is preserved by monotonic transformations of random variables

This allows us to use a neat trick of simulating from different marginals with a known degree of correlation

Suppose I know $\rho_{PQ} = -.25$

$$Q \sim \text{Beta}$$

$$P \sim \log - \text{Normal}$$

Process involves simulating from a multivariate normal with known degree of correlation — invert (to get uniform R.V) — then drop into desired marginal. This will yield correlated variables from the different marginal.

Process

1) Start with known correlation matrix

$$\text{e.g.} - \begin{bmatrix} 1 & \rho_{12} \\ \rho_{21} & 1 \end{bmatrix}$$

2) Take Cholesky decomposition — $P'\rho = \Sigma$
   where P = chol (Σ)
   Σ = correlation matrix
3) generated correlated standard normals —
   Say e ~ N (0, I)
   u = e*P ~ N (0, Σ)
4) Take cdf of these normals —
   V_i = cdf ('Normal', u_i, 0, 1)
5) Plug these values (which are uniform distributed) into quantile function of interest
   e.g. — y_i = quantile ('Beta', V_i, 5, 3) ∗ 221;
   This will yield y_i that has desired correlation matrix.
   One Minor Point —
   Spearman correlation + Pearson correlation have slightly different expectations —

$$\left.\begin{array}{r} r = \text{Spearman} \\ c = \text{Pearson} \end{array}\right\} c = 2 \cdot \sin\left(\frac{\pi}{6} \cdot r\right)$$

— A very brief note on time-varying price risk models — ARCH, GARCH, stochastic volatility
— often used to represent "risk" is econometric models (Holt has many important papers)
— Better suited to be covered in a finance course — but you should all be aware of these approaches.

Chapter 7

Stochastic Specification Issues in Empirical Models

Supplemental Notes/Review of Bootstrap

Data from sample "pulls itself up by bootstrap"

Suppose we have sample $X_1, \ldots, X_n$ —

If we know X_i drawn from $N(u, \sigma^2)$ — we know

95% CI for $\mu = \left[\bar{X} - 1.96\frac{\sigma}{\sqrt{N}}, \bar{X} + 1.96\frac{\sigma}{\sqrt{N}}\right]$

But what if it is not normal?

Or, what if instead of mean you were interested in a statistic whose distribution is unknown or difficult to evaluate — e.g., median X.50

Conventional notation —

For sample $X_1, \ldots, X_n$ n observations

If we resample m observations with replacement —

$X_1^*, \ldots, X_m^*$ = Bootstrap sample

$\bar{X}$ is mean of $X_1, \ldots, X_n$

$\bar{X}^*$ is mean of $X_1^*, \ldots, X_m^*$

Empirical, nonparametric bootstrap is resample of $m = n$ (resample same size sample)

For any statistic (function of data) θ, you can also calculate from bootstrap sample $= \theta^*$

The Bootstrap principle:

1) If original data drawn from $F(x)$ —
$F^*(x) \approx F(x) \Rightarrow$ Bootstrap sample approximates unknown distribution
2) Distribution of θ^* approximates distribution of θ (sometimes this approximation is not good — which is why we desire pivotal statistics).

Example — we want a confidence interval for true mean of distribution —

That is, we want to know distribution of

$$\delta = \overline{x} - \mu$$

If we know this distribution, we could find

$\delta_{.95} + \delta_{.05}$ "critical values" and construct a 90%

$$CI = prob\left(\delta_{.95} \leq \overline{x} = u < \delta_{.05} \mid \mu\right) = .90$$

on 90% $CI = \left[\overline{X} - \delta_{.05}, \overline{X} - \delta_{.95}\right]$

We don't know critical values $\delta_{.05}$, $\delta_{.95}$ because we don't know the distribution of δ

But — we can approximate it using

$$\delta^* = \overline{X}^* - \overline{X}$$

mean of	mean of
Bootstrap sample	sample

We compute $\delta^* = \overline{X}^* - \overline{X}$ B times, using resampling of n observations

Our bootstrap $CI = \left[\overline{X} - \delta^*_{.05}, \overline{X} - \delta^*_{0.95}\right]$

Note — we should have taken $\overline{X}^*$ B times and calculated $\overline{X}^*_{.05}, \overline{X}^*_{.95}$ — but this is not a pivotal statistic.

Definition — given a data vector, X, a random variable $Q(X, \theta)$ is a "Pivotal Quantity" if its distribution does not depend on unknown parameters.

Example — we want a $(1-\alpha)$ % confidence intend for θ that is a function of data but that does not depend on θ —

Suppose $X_1,\ldots, X_n$ is random sample from u $[0, \theta]$ — we want $(1-\alpha)$% CI for θ —

What transformation would free this from θ?

$$\text{Ans} - \frac{X_1}{\theta},\ldots,\frac{X_n}{\theta} \Rightarrow \text{pivotal quantity} \sim u[0,1]$$

So — we choose a + b such that

$$\text{prob}\left(a < \frac{X_{(n)}}{\theta} < b\right) = (1-\alpha)$$

Since $\text{prob}\left(a < \frac{X_{(n)}}{\theta} < b\right)$ — rearrange —

$$\text{p}_r\left(\frac{X_i}{b} < \theta < \frac{X_{(n)}}{a}\right)$$

Note: for $X_1,\ldots, X_n$ iid from f (x, θ),
if $\hat{\theta}$ = MLE estimate, then —

1) If θ is location parameter — $\hat{\theta} - \theta$ is pivotal quantity
2) If θ is scale parameter — $\hat{\theta}/\theta$ is pivotal

   If F (X, θ_1, θ_2) has both location = θ_1
   and scale = θ_2
   Then $\frac{(\hat{\theta}_1-\theta_1)}{\hat{\theta}_z}$ is a pivotal quantity for θ_1
   and $\hat{\theta}_2/\theta_2$ is pivotal for θ_2
   So — to summarize pivotal method —

1) Identify a pivot for parameter of interest
2) Identify the distribution of pivot quantity
3) Choose confidence interval based on quantiles of pivot distribution
4) Solve for the unknown parameter to get CI.

Sometimes a pivot does not exist, but we can get approximate or asymptotic pivot —

If $X_1,\ldots,X_n \sim F(X, \theta)$ and $T(X, \theta)$ is random variable depending only on $X + \theta - T(\cdot)$ is approximate pivot if its distribution is "approximately unchanged" when θ changes.

Asymptotic normality plays important role here.

Recall MLE estimate $\hat{\theta}$ has the property —

$$\sqrt{N}(\hat{\theta} - \theta_0) \xrightarrow{d} N(o, \Sigma)$$

Then $\sqrt{N\Sigma^{-1}}(\hat{\theta} - \theta)$ is approximate pivot for θ_0 since

$$\sqrt{N\Sigma^{-1}}(\hat{\theta} - \theta_o) \xrightarrow{d} N(o, I)$$

Horowitz shows that statistics that are not asymptotically pivotal do not provide "higher order approximation" to distribution — are only 1st order approx.

Returning to Percentile CI

Define $T_n^* = \hat{\theta} - \theta$

Construct B Replicates of T_n^* by bootstrap —

Sort T_n^*: $T_1^*, \ldots, T_B^*$

$$\text{Take } \frac{\alpha}{2} \text{ and } 1 - \frac{\alpha}{2} \text{ percentiles:}$$

$$CI = \left[\hat{\theta} - g_n^*\left(1 - \frac{\alpha}{2}\right), \hat{\theta} - g^*\left(\frac{\alpha}{2}\right)\right]$$

Applied to a test statistics — *t*-percentile —

Set $T_n(\theta) = (\hat{\theta} - \theta) / s(\hat{\theta})$

We reject $T_n(\theta_0) < C$ if $prob(T_n(\theta) < C) = \alpha$

So — calculate B replicates of $T_n^* = (\hat{\theta}^* - \hat{\theta}) / s(\hat{\theta}^*)$ BS t is centred at $\hat{\theta}$

Sort these to find $q_n^*(\alpha)$ and ln $q_n^*(1-\alpha)$

Calculate $T_n(\theta)$ from original data —

$$T_n(\theta) = (\hat{\theta} - \theta) \big/ s(\hat{\theta})$$

Compare $T_n(\theta)$ to sample of $T_n^*(\theta)$ —
if it exceeds $T_n^*(\theta^*) = 1-\alpha$, then reject.

Note — if I know underlying parametric distribution — could draw from it instead.

Percentile t confidence interval —
From replicates of $T_n^*\ldots$, get quantiles $T_n^*(\frac{\alpha}{2})$, $T_n^*(1-\frac{\alpha}{2})$
Percentile t confidence interval is then —

$$CI = \left[\hat{\theta} - \hat{S}(\theta) \cdot g_n^*(1-\alpha/2), \hat{\theta} - \hat{S}(\theta) \cdot g_n^*(\alpha/2)\right]$$

Note, for 95% CI for standard t – g* = –1.64,1.64

We can guarantee a symmetric t-percentile, by using absolute values —
Consider estimate of $|T_n^*| = |\hat{\theta}^* - \hat{\theta} / s(\hat{\theta}^*)|$
Then —

$$CI = \left[\hat{\theta} - S(\hat{\theta}) \cdot g_n^*(\alpha), \hat{\theta} + S(\hat{\theta}) \cdot g_n^*(\alpha)\right]$$

When/why Bootstrap?

1) we are unsure of underlying distribution
2) correcting bias in estimation
3) when it is impossible (or impractical) to derive true asymptotic distribution or calculate standard errors.

Assume output is random —

The Bootstrap (Hansen Ch.10) { Discuss different versions of sampling

Let F (·) denote a joint distribution function for a population of observations (x_i, y_i)

Let T_n be a statistic of interest (e.g. t – test)

$$T_n = T_n((x_1, y_1) \ldots,(x_n\ y_n), F)$$

The exact CDF of T_n when data are sampled from F is

$$G_n\ (u, F) = \text{Prob}\ (T_n \leq uF)$$

which demonstrates that G_n depends on $F(\cdot)$.

But in many cases, F is unknown,

We can approximate $G_n\ (\cdot)$ asymptotically with

$$G\ (u.\ F) = \lim_{n-\infty} G_n\ (u, F)$$

If G (·) does not depend on F, we say T_n is "asymptotically pivotal" and use $G\ (u)$ for inference

Efron (1979) proposed the bootstrap which makes a different approximation —

Unknown F replaced by a consistent estimate F_n.

Which yields $G^*_n\ (u) = G_n\ (U, F_n)$

↑Bootstrap Distribution

Let $(y^*\ x^*)$ represent random variables from F_n

A random sample from this distribution is a "bootstrap" sample.

$T^*_n = T_n\ ((y^*_1,x^*_1)\ldots,(y^*_n,x^*_n), F_n)$ is constructed from this sample.

T^*_n has distribution identical to T_n when F_n is true cdf.

Empirical Distribution Function (EDF)

Joint $F_n(y,x) = \frac{1}{n}\sum 1(y_i \leq y)1(x_i \leq x)$

F_n is step function — defines empirical quantiles

EDF consistently estimates CDF + is nonparametric

By WLLM $F_n(y,x) \xrightarrow{d} F(y,x)$

By CLT $\sqrt{n}\,(F_n(x,y) - F(x,y)) \xrightarrow{d} N(O, F(1-F))$

Nonparametric Bootstrap →

Uses EDF as estimate of $F(x, y)$

Uses resampling with replacement from sample of n observations

n_i is # random iid draws — $n_i = n$

Random pairs (vectors) drawn randomly (y^*, x^*) each has 1/n probability of being drawn.

For each replicated sample of n_i observations, the bootstrap test statistic is calculated.

$T_n^* = T_n((y_1^*, x_1^*) \ldots (y_b^*, x_b^*))$ — Done B times

B = # replicated samples.

BS statistic typically depends on F through parameter —

e.g. t-ratio $= (\hat{\theta} - \theta)/s(\hat{\theta})$ depends on θ

Using BS to Estimates Bias + Variance —

$Bias(\hat{\theta}) = E(\hat{\theta} - \theta_0)$

Let $T_n = E(T_n(\theta_0))$

For B bootstrap samples, calculate θ_i^* and

$$T_n^* = \hat{\theta}^* - \hat{\theta}$$

$$T_n^* = E(T_n^*) = \frac{1}{B}\sum_{i=1}^{B} T_{nb}^* = \frac{1}{B}\sum_{i=1}^{B} \hat{\theta}_b^* - \hat{\theta}$$

$$= \bar{\hat{\theta}}^* - \hat{\theta}$$

= A measure of bias in $\hat{\theta} = \hat{T}_n$

We could then use this to construct a bias — corrected estimates

$$\tilde{\theta} = \hat{\theta} - T_n \qquad \text{Bias correction } \tilde{\theta}^* = \hat{\theta} - \hat{T}_n$$

$$= \hat{\theta} - (\bar{\hat{\theta}}^* - \hat{\theta}) = 2\hat{\theta} - \bar{\hat{\theta}}^*$$

Let $T_n = \hat{\theta}$ and consider variance of $\hat{\theta}$

$V_n = E(T_n - ET_n)^2$

$$\text{So} - \hat{V}_n^* = \frac{1}{B}\sum_{i=1}^{B}\left(\hat{\theta}_b^* - \bar{\hat{\theta}}^*\right)^2$$

Bootstrap std. error = $\sqrt{\overline{Vn}^{*}(\hat{\theta})}$
Bootstrap percentile →
Define quantile function $g_n(\alpha, F)$ —
$g_n(\alpha, F)$ solves $G_n(g_n(\alpha, F), F) = \alpha$
where G_n is distribution function.
Define $g_n(\alpha)$ = "true" quantile
Define $g_n^{*}(\alpha) = g_n(\alpha, F_n)$ quantile function of bootstrap dist.
Let $T_n = \hat{\theta}$, a parameter of interest.
In $(1 - \alpha)$ % of samples $\hat{\theta}$ will be in region $\left[g_n(\alpha/2), g_n\left(1-\frac{\alpha}{2}\right)\right]$
Suggests a percentile confidence interval (Efron) —

$$C_1 = \left[g_n^{*}(\alpha/2), g_n^{*}\left(1-\frac{\alpha}{2}\right)\right] \text{ Percentile Confidence Interval}$$

(Note: for t $g_n = \pm 1.96 \cdot \hat{\sigma}$)
Very popular confidence interval estimate
Note it is invariant to positive monotonic transformations —
$f(\theta)$ = monotonically increasing $f(\cdot)$
then $\left[g_n^{*}(\alpha/2), g_n^{*}\left(1-\frac{\alpha}{2}\right)\right]$ same interval as $f(\theta)$.
C_1 can be rewritten as

$$C_1 = \left[\hat{\theta} + g_n^{*}\left(\frac{x}{2}\right), \hat{\theta} + g_n^{*}\left(1-\frac{\alpha}{2}\right)\right]$$

Note something here though — we are doing this because we don't know true underlying cdf.

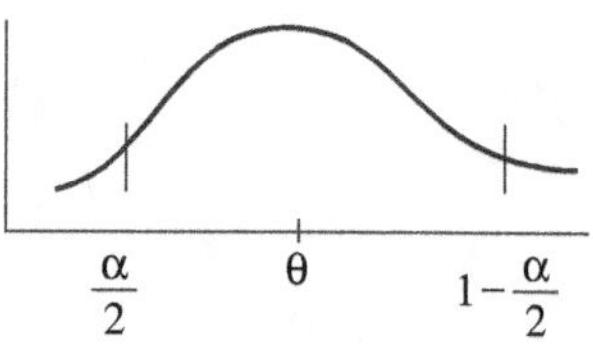

By defining CI by taking
We assume G (·) is symmetric
If G (·) is not symmetric — the bootstrap coverage level will not be $1 - \alpha$

So Efron's bootstrap percentile method should not be used unless underlying density is symmetric — or can be transformed to be symmetric.

An alternative method —
Sort replicates and pick $\left[\alpha/2, 1-\frac{\alpha}{2}\right]$ quantiles

e.g. — if $T_n = (\hat{\theta}^* - \hat{\theta})$ is statistic centered at $\hat{\theta}$,
Sort values of T_n to find $[T_n - g(\alpha/2), T_n - g(1-\alpha/2)]$
And, for example, 95% C.I. =

$$\left[\hat{\theta} - g_n^*(.975), \hat{\theta} - g_n^*(.025)\right]$$

Percentile — t Equal — Tailed interval —
Want to test H_0' $\theta = \theta_0$ vs H_a: $\theta < \theta_0$ at single α —
Set $T_n(\theta) = (\hat{\theta} - \theta)/s(\hat{\theta})$

If $T_n(\theta) < C \Rightarrow$ reject — where we choose C such that
prob $(T_n(\theta_0) < C) = \alpha$
So — C = quantile $g_n(\alpha)$
A bootstrap replaces $g_n(\alpha)$ with bootstrap estimate $g_n^*(\alpha)$ (from empirical quantile)
Test rejects if $T_n(\theta_0) < g_n^*(\alpha)$
Note that bootstrap sample is centered at $\hat{\theta}$ and $s(\hat{\theta})^*$ is calculated from bootstrap sample.
We can take the sorted simulated sample of $T_n^* = (\hat{\theta} - \theta)/s(\theta)$
And get a "percentile — t confidence interval" — smallest — largest →

$$T_1 \cdots T_i \cdots T_j \cdots T_n$$
$$g(\alpha/2) \quad g(1-\alpha/2)$$

Note — may not be symmetric
Sort T_i statistics $T_i = \frac{(\hat{\theta} - \theta)}{s(\theta)}$

$$T_1 \cdots\cdots T_{.95} \cdots T_{.999}$$

.05 (for 90% C.I.) and total

Then $\left[\hat{\theta} - s(\hat{\theta}) \cdot g_n(\alpha/2), \hat{\theta} + s(\hat{\theta}) \cdot g_n(\alpha/2)\right]$
Note — for conventional t with $\alpha = .10$, $g = 1.64$
Note that this bootstrapping approach can be done for other test statistics —

$$\text{e.g.} - \text{Wald Test} = w_n(\theta) = n(\hat{\theta} - \theta)\overset{\alpha}{\mathrm{V}}{}_{\theta}^{-1}(\hat{\theta} - \theta)$$

$$\xi$$

Bootstrap est.

There are other approaches to estimating confidences intervals
Consider bootstrapping in OLS setting —

1) Bootstrap from empirical distribution as above
2) Bootstrap from residuals ε_i — assumed to be iid —
   Estimation sample = $y_1,\ldots,y_n$
   $x_1,\ldots,x_n$

   Estimate: $\min_{\beta} y - g(\beta, X) \Rightarrow yields\,\hat{\beta}$

Then generate a "pseudo sample" by randomly sampling residents + adding to $\hat{y}$
- — Select $(\varepsilon_1^* \ldots, \varepsilon_n^*)$
- — Create bootstrap sample $y_1 + \varepsilon_1^*,\ldots, y_n + \varepsilon_n^*$
- — Repeat large # times

3) "Wild" Bootstrap — works well against heteroskedasticity
   Consider linear heteroskedastic model —
   $y_i = x_i\,\beta + \varepsilon_i$
   $E\,(\varepsilon_i\,\mathrm{x}_i) = 0$
   $E\,(\varepsilon_i^2\,x_i) = \sigma_i^2$
   With wild bootstrap, residuals are modified
   $u_i^* = h_i\,(\varepsilon_i)$ where h_i is a transformation
   For the heteroscedastic model — the suggested transformation is —

$$\left.\begin{array}{c} h_i(\hat{u}_i) = \hat{u}_i/(1 - H_i)^{1/2} \\ \text{or} \\ h_i(\hat{u}_i) = \hat{u}_i/(1 - H_i) \end{array}\right\} H_i = X_i(X_i'X)^{-1}X_i'$$

4) Parametric Bootstrap

If I am confident that I know the distribution of the estimation sample — I can sample from it instead —

e.g.– $Y_i = \alpha + B_1 X_{1i} + B_2 X_{2i} + u_i$

estimate by MLE (assume MVN: multivariate normal) —

generate $\hat{y} = \alpha + \hat{\beta}_1, X_{1i} + \hat{\beta}_2 X_{2i} + \hat{u}_i$

instead of residuals, sample from $N(0,\hat{\sigma}^2)$

5) Bootstrapping with dependent Data

(Block Bootstrapping)

Consider case of dependence

$$Y_{it} = \alpha_{it} + \beta_1 X_{it} + e_{it}$$
$$e_{it} = \rho\, e_{it-1} + V_{it} \qquad E(V_{it}) = 0, \sigma^2$$

Need to define "independent blocks" that can be sampled from —

In this case, I would sample from pairs of observations —

$$\begin{bmatrix} y_1, & x_{11} \\ y_2, & x_{12} \end{bmatrix}$$

When form of dependence is unknown, there are many ways to define blocks

— Overlapping

— Expanding radius

— Non overlapping blocks

— Active area of research

— etc.

Bootstrapping to obtain critical values —

Many problems are not amenable to conventional tests —

e.g.– structural break at unknown point —

conventional chow test inferences are not valid when using sup (F) to detect break point.

We can simulate test under the null (random sample from data with replacement) + generate critical values that the sample test statistic value can be compared to.

Frontier Production Functions + Technical Efficiency

(Betteze (1992) survey)

Due to Lowell + Schmidt

The idea — firms may be off their technically efficient frontier —

In relative input space —

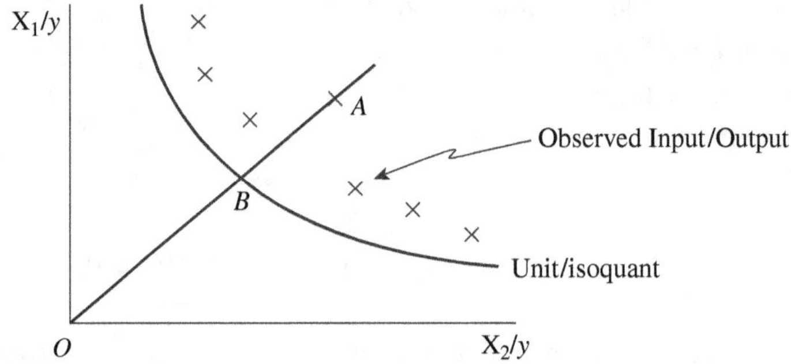

Technical efficiency = $^{OB}/_{OA}$

Or — in input/output space →

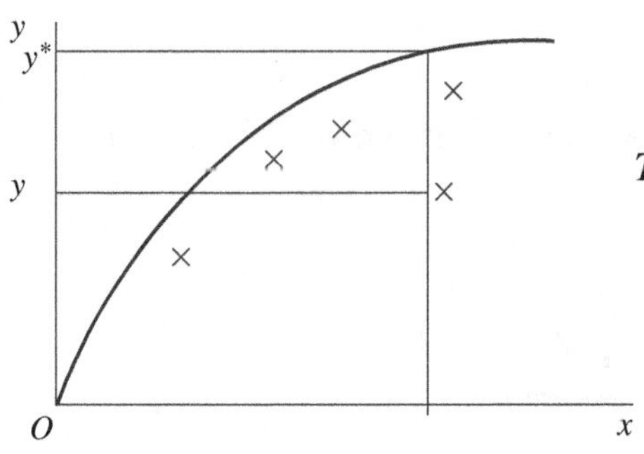

$TE = Y/Y^*$

TE = factor by which output is beneath its most efficient level.

$$TE = y_i/y_i^* = f(X_i, \beta) \exp(-u_i)/f(x_i, \beta)$$
$$= \exp(-u_i)$$

Where u_i is a one — sided (half — normal) or exponential error (can only be of a given sign).

Greene showed if the u_i terms are iid gamma MLE regularity conditions are satisfied —

stochastic frontier production function —

$$y = f(x_i, \beta) \exp(V_i - u_i) \qquad V_i = \text{mean 0 random variable}$$

So — $V_i \sim N(0, \sigma^2 v)$ and independent of u_i

Stochastic frontier prod. fn =

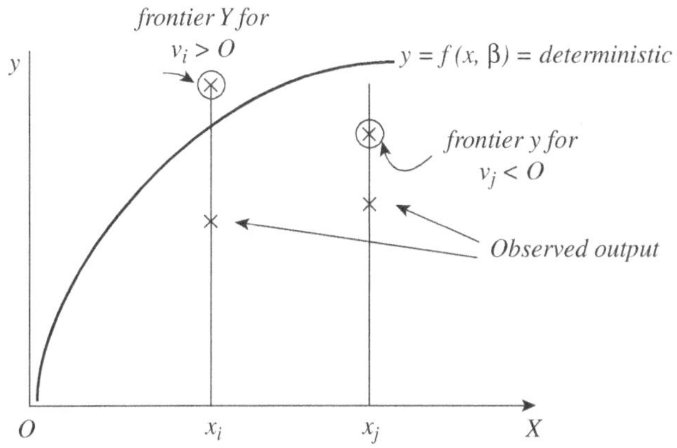

MLE obtained by assuming parameterization of $\sigma^2_v + \sigma^2_u$ — parameterize as $\lambda = \sigma^2_u / \sigma^2_v$ so that $\lambda > 0$

This allows MLE to identify

exp $(- u_i)$ = a measure of technical (in) efficiency

often conducted in a two-stage analysis where determinants of exp $(- u_i)$ are evaluated (e.g. policy)

Most application use panel data and thus the usual fixed/random effects issues become relevant

The next homework will includes an application

Realized output = expected output + random term —

$$y_t = \bar{y} + \varepsilon$$

For factor prices = r, inputs = x, agent actually minimizes following, cost problem —

$$\min \Sigma r.x + \qquad \text{s.t. } \overline{y} \geq E(f(x,\varepsilon))$$

We have touched on aspects of this before — (recall questions about how robust duality results are)

Several issues are relevant —

1) Ex Ante VS. Ex – post cost functions —

Remember — because of production lags, output is not known at time that production decisions are made.

The solution to this problem yields an "ex-ante" cost function — $\overline{c}(r,\overline{y})$

Problem is that, in empirical work, we observe y_t and not $\overline{y}$ and ε.

What if we ignore problem and use y_t instead of $\overline{y}$?

Pope and Just (1996) work through this problem for ex-ante translog cost function —

$$\ln \overline{c}(r,\overline{y}) = \alpha_0 + \alpha_r \ln r + \alpha_y \ln \overline{y} + \frac{1}{2}\beta_{rr}(\ln r)^2 + \frac{1}{2}\beta_{yy}(\ln \overline{y})^2 + \beta_{yn} \ln r \ln \overline{y}$$

Substitute $\overline{y} - y_t - \varepsilon$

$$\ln \tilde{c}(\cdot) = \alpha_0 + \frac{1}{2}\beta_{rr}(\ln r)^2 + \alpha_n \ln r + \alpha_y[\ln y - \ln \varepsilon] +$$

$$\beta_{yy}\left[\frac{1}{2}(\ln y)^2 + \ln y \ln \varepsilon + \frac{1}{2}(\ln \varepsilon)^2\right] + \beta_{yn}(\ln r)(\ln y - \ln \varepsilon)$$

Simplify this —

$$\ln \tilde{c}(\cdot) = \alpha_0 + \alpha_r \ln r + \alpha_y \ln y + \frac{1}{2}\beta_{rr}(\ln r)^2 + \frac{1}{2}\beta_{yy}(\ln y)^2 + \beta_{yn} \ln r \ln y + \varepsilon_0$$

Where $\varepsilon_0 = (-\alpha_y - \beta_{yr} ln_r - \beta_{yy} lny + \beta_{yy} ln\ \varepsilon)\ ln\ \varepsilon$

Use Shephard's lemma to derive shares —

$$\partial \ln \tilde{c} \big/ \partial \ln r = S = \alpha_r \beta_{rr} \ln r + \beta_{yr} \ln \bar{y}$$
$$= \alpha_r \beta_{rr} \ln r + \beta_{yr} \ln y + \varepsilon_1$$

Where $\varepsilon_1 = -\beta_{yr} \ln \varepsilon$

Typically, one would use GLS to estimate —

$$\ln \tilde{c}(r, \bar{y}) = \alpha_0 + \alpha_r \ln r + \alpha_y \ln y + \frac{1}{2} \beta_{rr} (\ln r)^2 +$$
$$\frac{1}{2} \beta_{yy} (\ln y)^2 + \beta_{yr} \ln r \ln y + \varepsilon_0 + u_0$$
$$\partial \ln \tilde{c} \big/ \partial \ln r = \alpha_r \beta_{rr} \ln r + \beta_{yr} \ln y + \varepsilon_1 + u_1$$

Where $u_0 + u_1$ are econometric estimation errors.

Problems — ε appears in ε_0, ε_1, and y

Thus regressors are correlated with errors

— endogeneity bias

— inconsistency

How to address this — standard approach — IV —

We need something correlated with y but not $\varepsilon_0 + \varepsilon_1$

Available instruments include r and x — but they both are correlated with ε_0

Using x as instrument only in estimating share equation will yield consistent estimate — but this is inefficient and may prove uninformative.

Pope and Just's Suggested Solution

— Use observed *x*,*y*, + *r* along with assumption about parametric form of the cost function to calculate $\bar{y}$

— Then we have $\bar{y}$ and can use it to estimate parameters of cost fn.

We must ask — what was agent trying to produce? (what was their $\bar{y}$)? Suppose we assume agents technology is represented by a generalized Leontief Ex Ante cost function —

$$\tilde{c}(\cdot) = \varphi(\bar{y})(r^{1/2})'\beta(r^{1/2})$$

Where $\varphi(\bar{y})$ is some function of $\bar{y}$ and, for 2 input case,

$$r^{1/2} = \left[r_1^{1/2} r_2^{1/2}\right], \beta = \begin{bmatrix} \beta_{11} & \beta_{12} \\ \beta_{21} & \beta_{22} \end{bmatrix}$$

Example of $\varphi(\cdot) = \ln(\bar{y})$

Assuming efficient production and non-random prices — we can solve for agent's explicit output, since we know —

$$\tilde{c}(r, \bar{y}, B) = r'x$$

Just and Pope adopt a distance function argument that also will allow for unobserved factor prices —

$$y = \max_{\bar{y}} \left\{ \bar{y} \mid \min_{r} \left[1 - \tilde{c}(r, \bar{y}, B) + r'x\right] \geq 1 \right\}$$

This adds one additional layer to the search if prices are not known —

If prices are not known — search over all prices until your find set of prices that puts observed inputs on isoquant for given level of expected output.

(– choose prices to may be sure distance function value = 1)

If prices are observed , do not need this extra step.

Example — Leontief technology: y = min $[\gamma_1 x_1, \gamma_2 x_2] + \varepsilon$

— if I know γ_i's and you told me what the x_i's were, I could easily tell you $\bar{y}$

— In this case, as long as I know cost min behavior holds, I only need one x_i

Consider 2 price Generalized Leontief example —

$\bar{y} = \varphi^{-1}\left(\frac{1}{\mu}\right)$ Where μ is largest characteristic root of —

$$\begin{bmatrix} \dfrac{\beta_{11}}{X_1} & \dfrac{\beta_{12}}{X_1^{1/2} X_2^{1/2}} \\ \dfrac{\beta_{12}}{X_1^{1/2} X_2^{1/2}} & \dfrac{\beta_{22}}{X_2} \end{bmatrix}$$

(Note — for $\phi(y) = y$ and $\beta_{12} = 0$, this reduces to standard Leontief and we just use largest diagonal element

To estimate — plug $\bar{y}$ into GL form —

$$\tilde{c}(\cdot) = \varphi\left(\varphi^{-1}\left(1/\bar{\mu}\right)\right) r^{1/2'} \beta r^{1/2} = \frac{1}{\bar{\mu}} r^{1/2'} \beta r^{1/2}$$

And then minimizing sum squared errors, unless $\bar{\mu}$ is a non-linear calculation for each data point prior to minimization of SSE

One can apply nonlinear least squares to recover consistent estimate of β

— but we do not need to recover φ as it drops out when we plug in $\bar{\mu}$

Just + Pope recommend adding another equation to estimation system —

$$y_t = \varphi^{-1}\left(\frac{1}{\bar{\mu}}\right)\varepsilon_t$$

Pope + Just consider a Monte Carlo exercise to compare different estimations —

They find that both ex-ante + expost gives biased estimate but that ex-ante is consistent

Bias + MSE of ex ante always smaller then expost

As variance of ε rises, y_t becomes worse proxy for $\bar{y}$

Moschini's 2001 (J. Econometrics) Critique

Recall that Pope + Just estimate just one of the two following systems —

$$c_t = \left(\frac{1}{\overline{\mu}_t}\right) r_t^{1/2'} \beta r_t^{1/2} + u_t$$

$$y_t = \varphi^{-1}\left(\frac{1}{\overline{\mu}_t}\right)\varepsilon_t$$

Or —

from McElroy's AGE model (see paper)
$$\begin{cases} C_t = \left(\frac{1}{\hat{\mu}}\right)\left(r_t^{1/2'} \beta r_t^{1/2} + t\alpha\, r_t\right) + r_t u_t \\ X_t = \left(\frac{1}{\hat{\mu}}\right)\left(r_t^{1/2} \beta r_t^{-1/2} + t\alpha\right) + u_t \end{cases}$$

When $\overline{\mu}$ is normal root of $\begin{bmatrix} \frac{\beta_{11}}{X_1} & \frac{\beta_{12}}{X_1^{1/2} X_2^{1/2}} \\ \frac{\beta_{12}}{X_1^{1/2} X_2^{1/2}} & \frac{\beta_2}{X_2} \end{bmatrix}$

Which we can write as $\overline{\mu}(x)$

Note a problem here — unless X is exogenous, expected output $\overline{y}_t$ will not be exogeneous since it is function of X — so X appears on both sides of the equation

Moschini's Solution

- — Broaden scope and assume that producers are profit maximizing
- — Use observed output price as an instrument for unobserved expected output
- — Can use assumption of functional form for *ex ante* cost function to solve P = MC for $\overline{y}$
- — plug this expression for $\overline{y}$ into problem rather than Pope + Just approach that depends on X's.

Example — CES Ex — Ante cost function

$$c(\cdot) = \overline{y}^{\beta}\left(\sum_i \alpha_i w_i^{1-\sigma}\right)^{\frac{1}{1-\sigma}} + \sum w_i e_i$$

Where w_i e_i corresponds to McElroy's AGEM that Pope + Just used
Derived Demand functions are —

$$x_i = \alpha_i \bar{y}_i^{\beta} w_i^{-\sigma} \left(\sum_k \alpha_k w_k^{1-\sigma} \right)^{\frac{1}{1-\sigma}} + e_i$$

Solve this for $\bar{y}$ as a function of X_i's (as is done by Pope + Just) —

$$\bar{y} = g(x - e, \theta) = \left(\sum_i \alpha_i^{1/\sigma} (X_i - e_i)^{(\sigma - 1)/\sigma} \right)^{\frac{\sigma}{\beta(1-\sigma)}}$$

Or, alternatively Moschini notes you can invoke f.o.c with respect to output ($P = MC$) and solve for $\bar{y}$ as a function of P —

$$\bar{y} = S(p, w, Q) = \left(\frac{p}{\beta} \right)^{\frac{1}{\beta - 1}} \left(\sum \alpha_i w_i^{1-\sigma} \right)^{\frac{1}{(1-\sigma)(\beta-1)}}$$

Plug this back into expression for Xi's —

$$X_i = \alpha_i \left(\frac{p}{\beta} \right)^{\frac{\beta}{(\beta - 1)}} w_i^{-\sigma} \left(\sum_i \alpha_k w_k^{1-\sigma} \right)^{[1/(1-\sigma)]\left[\frac{\sigma + \beta}{1-\beta}\right]}$$

Moschini conducts a Monte Carlo simulation to evaluate + compare — finds —

— His approach yields less bias + better fit
— A surprise — ex post estimates is next best

Chapter 8

Damage Control + Pesticides

Seminal paper — Lichtenberg + Zilberman (1986)

Pope + Just specification that we discussed (allowing for additive + multiplicative risk) —

$$y = f_1(x) + f_2(x) \cdot e \qquad\qquad E(e) = 0$$

Shortcoming of this — arrived at allowing inputs to reduce variance — which implies a type of symmetry and is a restrictive view of how inputs can address risk.

An alternative but potentially more attractive view involves inputs as follows.

"Damage Control Agents"

Examples — pesticides, Herbicides, fungicides, frost control measures flood control, etc.

How do these function? —

— Reduce variances, also —
— Ensure maximum potential output is achieved

One issue that often arises is adaptability or immunity to controls (resistance)

L+Z (1986) note that previous work on damage control adopted common, standard types of specification applied in production analysis e.g. — Cobb Douglas

However — may not be suitable for damage control

— leading to substantial biases (generally result in biases upward of marginal productivity).

Common Approach

Define g (Z) = an abatement function

And production is written as —

$$t = f\,(X,\ g\,(Z))$$

where $f\,(x,\,1)$ = maximum potential output

$f\,(x,\,0)$ = maximum output that can be obtained if damages are at their maximum (not necessarily zero).

An equivalent approach works with a "damage function" —

$$y = f\,(x) \cdot (1 - D\,(n))$$

where $f\,(x)$ = max. potential output as function of usual inputs not related to damage control

$D\,(n)$ = damage function (% of lost output) which is function of n = pest population

For this case, abatement function may be written as —

$$n = h\,(n_0,\ Z,\ A)$$

n_0 = initial pest population

Z = level of pesticide

A= possible alternative pest control method

$$h'_x < 0$$
$$h'_n < 0$$

Examples of abatement function — $g\,(z)$ —

Exponential = $g\,(z) = (1 - \exp\,(-\lambda z))$

Weibull = $g\,(z) = 1 - \exp\,(-z^{\alpha})$

Logistic = $(1 + \exp\,(\mu - \sigma z))^{-1}$

Any cdf

All assume shapes like —

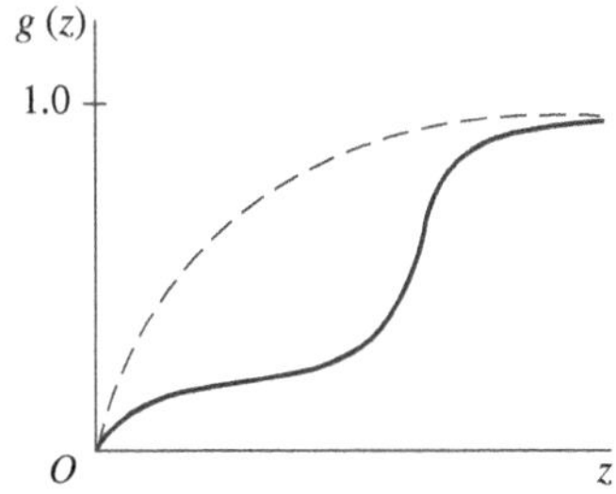

Lets consider optimization problem —

$$t = f(x, g(z))$$

2 types of problem — (equivalent)

1) Choose level of abatement services —

$$\max_{x,g} \quad \Pi = -p \cdot f(x,g) - r \cdot x - s \cdot g$$

$$S = \text{price of unit abatement}$$

foc = $p. f'x = r$ soc = $F_{XX} \leq 0,\ F_{GG} \leq 0$

$p.f'g = s$ $F_{XX}\,F_{GG} - F_{XG}^{\;2} \geq 0$

yields optimal level of abatement (and such parameters as elasticity of demand for abatement)

This solution yields elasticity of demand for abatement — $\epsilon_G = \left[\frac{F_{GG} \cdot G}{F_G} - \frac{F_{Gx}^2\, G}{F_G F_{XX}}\right]^{-1}$

Or, equivalently, choose level of abatement inputs

$$\max_{x,z} \quad p \cdot f(x, g(z)) - r.x - s.Z$$

foc = $p\,f_x = r$ soc = $F_{XX} \leq 0$

$p.f_{g'}.\underbrace{g\,(z)}_{\partial G/\partial Z} = s$ $F_{GG}\,g^2 + F_G\,g' \leq 0$

$F_{XX}\,(F_{GG}g^2 + F_G g') - F_{XG}g^2 \geq 0$

Note soc will require $g'_z < 0$ (diminishing marginal product of z in providing abatement)

Solution yields elasticity of demand for damage control inputs $\epsilon_z = \left[\frac{n_G}{\epsilon_G} + n_g\right]^{-1}$ where $n_G = gZ / G$

$$n_g = g'Z / g$$

Models will predict —

— pesticide use increases with —

— increase in P (output price)

— increase in $g(Z)$ (potential output)

— increase in price of alternate controls

— increase in initial population n_0

— decrease in price of abatement input S

— increase in price of alternate control methods

$L + Z$ discuss economic implications of these models —

1) Marginal effectiveness curve is elastic for most levels of Z

$$\Rightarrow \left|n_g\right| = \left|\frac{\partial G}{\partial Z} \cdot \frac{Z}{g}\right| > 1$$

   — Increasing Z by 1% usually causes abatement to fall by more than 1% (may not hold for all functional forms)

2) Demand for damage control inputs is inelastic almost everywhere —

$$\in_Z = \left|\frac{\partial Z}{\partial s} \cdot \frac{s}{Z}\right| < 1$$

   This is driven by elasticity of effectiveness

3) Demand for abatement and demand for damage control inputs are 2-sides to same coin

   — If demand for abatement in perfectly inelastic, demand for damage control inputs is perfectly inelastic

We can show — $\in_Z = \frac{\in_G}{n_G + n_g \cdot \in_G}$

So — if $\in_G = 0 \Rightarrow \in_Z = 0$

LZ compare two competing Cobb — Douglas specification of empirical models.

A) $t = \alpha + \beta \ln x + \gamma \ln G(Z) + u$ {their idea}
B) $t = \alpha + \beta \ln x + \gamma \ln Z + u$ {standard}

Note — A — models structure of damage control
They show that, for (B) —
α = intercept = inconsistent + biased downward
γ = marginal abatement productivity parameter =
— inconsistent + biased upward = leads to overestimation of marginal productivity of damage control inputs Z.

Visual differences →

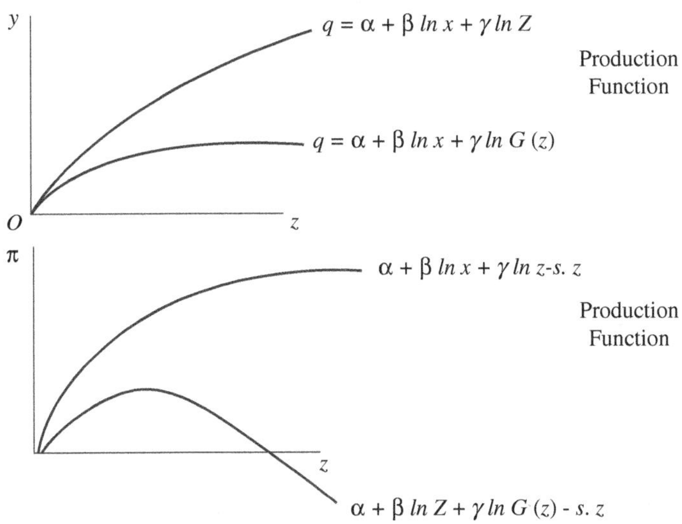

Previous literature on pesticide demand find that —

— farmers used too little pesticide
— MVP of pesticides 13x market price of pesticides.

LZ spend lots of time working out estimation issues for different specifications of damage function

Resistance Issues

Problem takes on dynamic issues when we consider possibility that pests may develop resistance over time (with cumulative use)

This leads to a shift in $g(z)$ as time/use accumulates — for same Z — more damage occurs —

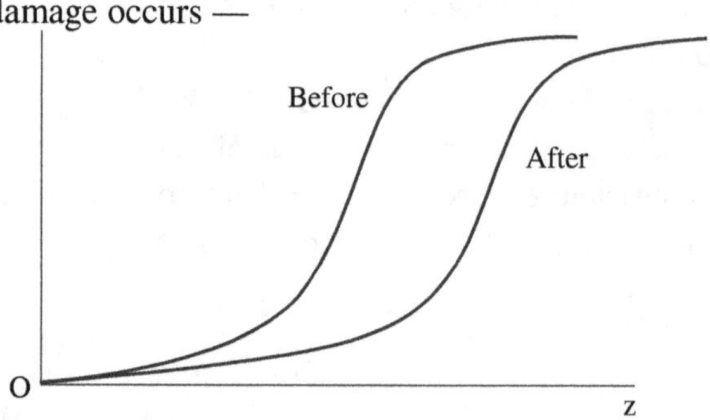

This implies marginal effectiveness function also shifts outward and that, with resistance, more pesticides are used.

Other Relevant Papers

1) Chambers + Lichtenberg, AJAE, 1994 —
   - — Derive dual representation for technologies with damage control elements
   - — Derive in a multiple — product setting
   - — Utilize "restricted profit" function — which is defined conditionally for given level of abatement
   - — Structure implies "conditional additively" —
     - — Prices of damage control inputs do not interact with prices of other inputs/outputs
     - — Simplifies profit — max solution
   - — Discuss econometric issues in estimation

— Apply to U.S. ag. data (aggregate) — using
  — Generalized Leontief restricted profit function
  — Logistic/exponential damage control function
— Final abatement is very inelastic to changes in use of other inputs (as LZ predicted)
— Conventional approaches that use pesticides as input yield every sign on elasticity

2) Saha, Summary, Havenner, AJAE 1997 —
   — Allow pesticides to have interactive effects with other productive inputs.

They note —

— Effectiveness of pesticides often depend on levels of moisture
— Fertilizer makes more weeds grow — thus limiting herbicide effectiveness.
— They allow specification with interactions between pesticides + other inputs in G (Z) function
— Test for 2 different types of shocks —
  — General production shock
  — Shock to effectiveness of damage control
— Use farm-level KS data
  — Cobb-Douglas production function
  — Modified exponential for G (·)
— They find support for interactive specification
  — Interaction between fertilizer + pesticides
    — Fertilizer decreases marginal effectiveness of pesticides
    — But, total MP still positive
— Support for error structure with errors in both damage control + regular production
— Specification yields smaller MP for pesticide + fertilizer
— Larger variance of MP for fertilizer + pesticide

Chapter 9

Time Allocation + Off-Farm Labor Supply

Some Facts About US Agriculture

— On-farm population has fallen steadily for last 100 yrs.
— Agriculture share of GDP approaching 1% (steady fall)
— Agriculture labor only 3.8% of "rural" population
— Very substantial dependence on off-farm work —
— For "average" farm — vast bulk of total household income is from off farm
— Even for "large commercial" family farms — about 40% of total Households income comes from off-farm work
— Observations —
— For any economy — development has implied a "migration" off the farm
— 2 ways to "migrate"–
1) Move to the city
2) Work off the farm

Other facts about US agriculture —
—farm sizes getting bigger } migration of
— number of farms } resources
Number of farms falling

Summer 1982 AJAE

Non-work time = leisure = yields utility
Work time — generate —

- — increases expected income
- — reduces risk of income
- — develops skill, experience, etc. to raise future income
- — directly affects utility

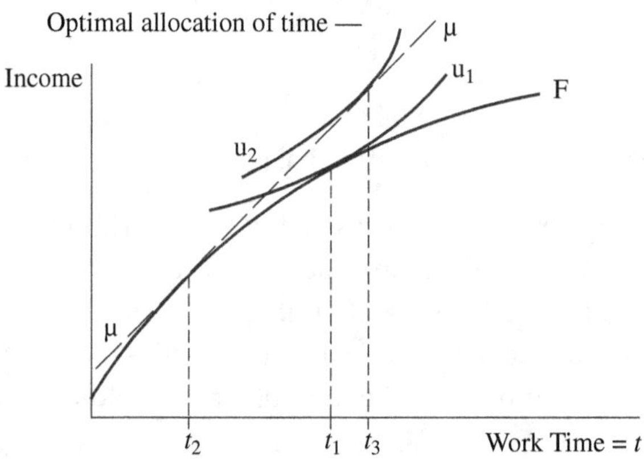

F = production function (*p)

M = off-farm labor market earnings function (slope = w_m = off-farm wage)

$\partial F/\partial_t = w_t$ = Marginal farm earnings function (falls due to diminishing, max utility)

With no off-farm work allowed — farmer works t_1, hours and reaches utility u.

Allow off-farm work — farmer can trade off farm labor for non-farm labor at positive rate —

Overall effort rises to t_3 — but farm work falls to t_2

$O–t_2$ = farm labor
$t_3–t_2$ = non-farm labor
t_3 = total labor

Note — marginal utility of leisure could imply less overall work (income effect)

Note — higher wage rate — more likely this will be.

This can yield backward bending supply.

Simple Analytical Model

Farm income = F(t_f, p_r, k, H_f)

t_f = farmer's work time

p_r = input + output prices

k = fixed inputs

H_f = farmer's human capital

$\frac{\partial^2 F}{\partial t_f^2} = w_f(t_f, p_v, k, H_f)$ = marginal farm wage

We expect $\frac{\partial^2 F}{\partial t_f^2} < 0$

$\partial w_f / \partial H_f > 0$ (if capital is "good")

Off-farm earnings = M = M(t_m, L_m, Z_m, H_m)

t_m = off-farm labor effect

L_m = labor market conditions (determine wage)

Z_m = job characteristics

H_m = skill + experience of worker

$w_m = \partial m / \partial t_m = w_m(L_m, Z_m, H_m)$ {Assumes no overtime

Non Work Time (Leisure)

$$u = u(t_u, g, X_u)$$

t_u = time spent on non work activities

g = consumption goods

x_u = fixed prices + household characteristics affecting utility

$w_u = MRS_{tug}$ = MRS time + goods in utility

$$w_u = \frac{\partial u / \partial t_u}{\partial u / \partial g} = w_u(t_u, g, X_u) = \text{slope of indifference curve}$$

Other issues — work today may contribute to productivity in the future (skill + experience).

e.g. farm experience ⇒ higher H_f in future

⇒ raises futures productivity

Uncertainty of wages (considered by Mishra and Goodwin)

Utility from work — some direct utility may result from farming

Taxes may be relevant (agriculture may be given more favourable taxation)

Time Allocation

Agents max u s.t. 2 constraints:

$G = F + M + Y$ = Budget constraint

(y = nonlabor income)

$t_u + t_f + t_m = T \Rightarrow$ Time constraint

Optional allocation will equalize all marginal values —

$$W_u = W_f = W_m$$

Criterion for off-farm work — ($t_m > 0$)

If $w_m > w_f(t_f^{**})$ where t^{**}_f = optimal hours of farm work if $t_m = 0$

t_f^{**} solves equality —

$$\mathrm{W}_u (T - t_f) = W_f (t_f)$$

So — we may want to consider model of off-farm work/non-work decision (discrete choice) —

$$D_m = D_m (X_u, Y, P_r, K, H_f, L_m, Z_m, H_m)$$
$$D_m = 1 \text{ if } t_m > 0$$
$$0 \text{ otherwise}$$

Or — to derive an "hours of work function"

$$t_m = t_m (X_u, Y, P_r, K, h_f, W_m) \qquad \leftarrow W_m \text{ observable if } t_m > 0$$

Empirical Analysis

1971 farm level survey (IL) — 822 farmers

3 steps to analysis — 1) profit of work/no-work
2) wage function
3) level of profit for work subsample

For # 2 + 3 — tested for selection bias — none found

Results

— Quadratic participation — peaks @ 43 yrs. (life cycle)
— Education raises off-farm work probability
— Training raises off-farm work
— Farming experience lower off-farm work (age affect)
— Local labor market matters — distance to farm
— # children + spouse education ⇒ no effect
— $ farm non-labor activities lowers off-farm work (wealth/income effect on leisure)
— Wage equation — education + experience raise wages

Huffman + Lange 1986 RESTAT

Extends Sumner analysis to consider nonnegativity constraints —

This is difficult econometrics problem — structure of husband's work decision is endogenous to wife's + vice versa.

Setting is farm family household — two individuals

— husband = M
— wife = F

Each receives endowment of time = $\bar{T}$/year.

Which is allocated:

$$\bar{T} = T_f^i + T_m^i + T_h^i \geq 0,\ i = M,F$$

f = farm work
m = market work
h = household time

Income is used on consumption goods = y
Net farm income = $p_q \cdot Q - WX$
Q = farm output $\quad$ p_q, W = output/input prices
X = inputs

Budget constraint —

$$W^m \cdot T^m_m + W^F T^f_M + p_q \cdot Q - WX + V = p_y \cdot Y$$

V = nonlabor income
Labor demand yields wage functions
$W^i = W^i(E^i, \psi)$ $\quad$ ψ = labor market condition
E^i = skills, education
Technology of farm production represented by —
$Q = Q(T^m_f, T^F_f, X, E^m, E^F, \Psi)$ {substitute into budget constraint
X = inputs
E^i = human capital, $i = M, F$
Household utility — (Note — @ household level)

$$u = u(T^m_h, T^F_h, Y, E^m, E^F, \Gamma)$$

$$\partial u/\partial \Omega > 0 \qquad \partial^2 u/\partial \Omega^2 < 0$$

$$\Omega = T^M_n, T^F_n, Y$$

Key variables = T^m_m, T^F_m = off-farm labor supply
These are jointly determined with x, T^i_f, T^i_h, Y

A common assumption — $MPT_f \to \infty$ as $T_f \to 0$ and $MU_y \to \infty$ as $Y \to 0$ — this allows us to assume interior solutions for these.

Problem — max u (·)

$$\text{S.t.} - W^m T^m_m + W^F T^F_m + P_q \cdot Q(\cdot) - WX + V - P_y Y = 0$$
$$T^i_f + T^i_m + T^i_h = \bar{T},\ T^i m \geq 0$$

FOC's (assume interior solutions for all but T^i_m)

$$\lambda(P_q Q_x - W) = 0 \qquad (7)$$

$$\lambda p_q QT'^i_f - \gamma^i = 0 \qquad (8)$$

$$\left.\begin{array}{l} \lambda w^i - \gamma^i \leq 0 \\ T_m^{\,i} > 0,\ T^i_m(\lambda w^i - \gamma^i) = 0 \end{array}\right\} \qquad (9)$$

$$u_{T^i_m} - \gamma_i = 0 \qquad (10)$$

$$u_y - \lambda p_y = 0 \qquad (11)$$

$$T - T^i_f - T^i_m - T^i_h = 0 \qquad (12)$$

(8)–(10) yield optional time allocations

(9) determines off-farm work —

If $W^i < \gamma^i/\lambda$ — then $T'^i_m{}^* = 0 \Rightarrow$ No work

If $W^i = \gamma^i/\lambda$ — individuals off-farm wage equals marginal value of home time + farm labour

If $T'^i_m > 0$ — (7)–(9) can be solved for profit max input use on the farm + this solution will be independent of other equations

But — when nonnegativity constraint is binding farm production decisions cannot be separated from household consumption + time allocation decisions —

If both husband + wife work off farm, —

$$T^i_m = \quad \overline{T} - T^{i*}_f - T^{i*}_h = S_i(W^m, W^F, W, P_q, P_y, V, E^m, E^f, \Psi, \Gamma)$$

But, if $T^{i\,*}_m = 0$ — then for i's spouse —

$T^{j\,*}_m = S'_i(W^j, W, P_q, \ldots, \Psi, \Gamma) \leftarrow$ note absence of w^i!

So — a "switching" regime type model is implied in this situation

Econometric Model

4 structural equations consisting of —

— labor demand (wage equations)

— off-farm labor supply

Labor demand : $W^i = X^i\ \beta^i + V^i$ if $W^i > W^{iR}$ Reservation Wage
For Male — labor supply =

$$T^m_m = W^m a^m_{11} + W^F a^m_{12} + Z^m\alpha + \mu^m \text{ if } W^m \geq W^{mR} \text{ and } W^F \geq W^{FR}$$
$$T^m_m = W^m a^{m*}_{11} + Z^m\alpha^* + \mu^{m*} \text{ if } W^m \geq W^{mR} \text{ and } W^F < W^{FR}$$
$$T^m_m = 0 \text{ otherwise (i.e., if } W^m < W^{MR})$$

So — structure shifts according to work decisions (endogenous switching)

Reservation wage is a function of exogenous variables and random distribution of spouse and nonwage exogeneous variables + random disturbance of labor supply $w^{iR} = \left(\frac{1}{a^i_{kk}}\right)\left(X^j\beta^j a^i_{kl} + Z\alpha^i + \mu^i + V^\alpha a^i_{kl}\right)$

Each of the regimes' probabilities can be modeled using bivariate probit models —

e.g. — $Pr\ (W^m > W^{mR},\ W^F > W^{FR})$
$= \rho_1\ (Z\theta_1^m, + X\theta_2^m, Z\theta_1^F + X\theta_2^F, \delta) = \rho_1$
↑ Correlation coefficient

These probit models, along with off-farm labor supply equations are used to form a multi-equation endogenous switching model.

Model simplified a little by recursive nature — market demand fit to those who have $T_m > 0$

H + L estimate this for survey sample of Iowa farms. Results conform to expectations —

— more schooling ⇒ more off-farm work
— husbands with early farm experience ⇒ less work
— young children ⇒ less off-farm work
— longer growing season ⇒ less off-farm work for farmer, no effect for wife
— larger asset income ⇒ less off-farm work
— longer commute ⇒ less off-farm work

Off-farm labor supply equations for using a major estimation (questionable)

Structures differ across regimes

Mishra + Goodwin — 1997, AJAE

— Often argued that off-farm work is a diversification strategy used to manage risk.
— Thus, we expect riskier farms should work more off-farm (risk measured with a lag).
— M + G consider this — note that risk aversion could drive a wedge between on-farm + off-farm wages
— Use KSU data — survey of farms
— Higher CV of historical income ⇒ Higher probability of off-farm work
— Also consider endogeneity of joint labor supply decisions using endogenous Tobit models

Ahituv + Kimhi — JDE — 2002

Endogenizes farm structure (in farm capital investment) to labor supply decisions

Common approach — $y_i = f(X_i, Z_i)$

Where Z_i = farm structure variables

A + K note that structure may change with off-farm labor supply decisions — raising an endogeneity concern. Z_i is endogenous to y_i

⇒ endogeneity of farm capital stock —

— for farms subject to borrowing constraints, increase in off-farm income may raise farm capital accumulation
— better off-farm earning opportunities may increase use of capital-intensive technologies (especially in developing countries)
— off-farm labor + capital accumulation may be closely related in life cycle

Analysis is to panel of Israeli farms using multinomial probit (no work, part time, full-time) together with switching regression model of farm capital.

Model — choose values of $K_t + L_t$ for $t = 1,\ldots,T$

$$\text{to max } E_t \sum_{t=1}^{T} \left(\frac{1}{1+r}\right)^t \left(AW_t^c h_t^c L_t + p_t f(A, h_t^f, K_t, 1-L_t, \theta_t) - p_t^1 I\right)$$

$$\begin{aligned} s.t. \qquad K_{t+1} &= I_t + (1-\delta)K_t \\ h_{t+1}^c &= L_t + h_t^c \\ h_{t+1}^f &= (1-L_t) + h_t^f \end{aligned}$$

where A = intrinsic ability
h^c = off-farm human capital
h^f = on-farm human capital
W^c = off-farm wage rate
$f()$ = prod. fn for farm output
I_t = capital investment
$0 < L < 1 \Rightarrow L = 1$ only off-farm work
δ = physical K depreciation

FOC —

$$p_t f_k(\cdot) = p_{t-1}^I (1+r) - p_t^I (1-\delta)$$

$$\left(\frac{1}{1+r}\right) + AW_t^c h_t^c + E_t \sum_{j=t+1}^{T} \left(\frac{1}{1+r}\right)^j AW_j^c L_j$$

$$= \left(\frac{1}{1+r}\right)^t p_t f(1-2(*)) + E_t \left(\frac{1}{1+r}\right)^j p_j f_h^f(j)$$

Data — 2 Censuses of Agriculture — 1971 + 1981

Econometric analysis is combination of multinomial probit and endogenous switching with random effects.

Estimate two versions of models — one where results for 1981 are "state dependent" on 1976 results (this is preferred specification)

— Confirm many of typical effects — age, education etc — find important life cycle effects in work decisions — work profitability peaks @ age 47

— Find that value of firms capital stock depends on off-farm work decisions (structural model varies across different work structures)
— For example — life cycle effects on farm capital stock vary according to work decisions
  — full time farmers invest more in farms' capital
— One issue to me — assume farm size is exogenous (capital stock only reflects buildings, machinery, equipment, livestock)

Kislev + Peterson 1982 JPE

Consider endogeneity of farm structure

— out migration of farm labor } closely linked
— growth of farm size }

Outmigration of labor = industry adjustment
farm size adjustment = firm adjustment
Construct model of equilibrium of farm size —
Determined by —

— input prices
— nonfarm income
— technology

Assume a fixed quantity of farm family labor —

— single farmer with no hired labor ($L = 1$)
— increasing machine size reflects technological progress and induced innovation
— increase in K/L occurs with adoption of bigger and more powerful machines
— one farm output (food)
— 2 level production process —
  f_m = mechanical = K + L combined to produce mechanical services = M (machines)
  f_B = biological land (A) + biological inputs (B)

So — per farm output = y =

$$Y = f(f_m\ (K,L),\ f_B(A,B))$$

Which we will consider as occurring in two stages —

$$Y = f(f_b\ (A,\ B,\ f_m\ (K,L))$$

They further rewrite this by defining A as being "augmented" by machines —

$$Y = H(A,B) \qquad A = \text{augmented with } f_m$$

Assume CRS + that machines/land rates = m is constant

This implies farm size is directly determined by number of machines produced.

$$A = {}^{M}\!/_{m}$$

W = wage = opportunity cost of farm labor

u = cost of machine services

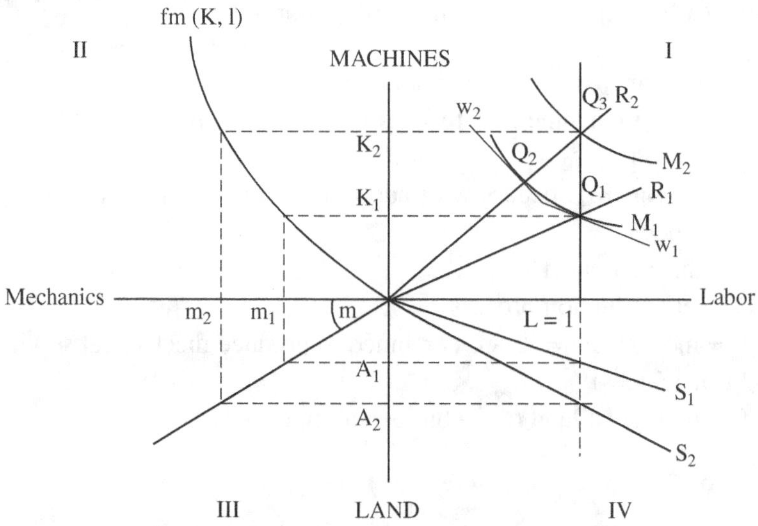

At price ratio w_I — family farm with L =1 will operate @ Q_1 — purchasing M_1 units of mechanics

For II — mechanics per unit labor production function is illustrated

For III — mechanics + land are combined in fixed proportions, IV = farm size (land/labor) notes.

Now — if prices shift $w_1 \rightarrow w_1$ — optimal output of mechanic changes $M_1 \rightarrow M_2$ farm size shifts $S_1 \rightarrow S_2$

Empirical Analysis — considers farm size changes over 1930–1970 period

Estimate single elasticity of substitution between $K + L$ using demand for labor —

$$y = \alpha + \beta w_f + e$$

y = value added per unit of labor
W_f = agricultural wage rate
$\beta = K/L$ e.o.s

They find that ratio of farm labor opportunity cost to price of machinery services almost perfectly explains changes in U.S. farm sizes 1930–1970.

Chapter 10

Survey of Current Farm Policy Issues

Great (slightly dated) overview paper on "the Farm Problem" by Gardner (JEL 1992)

The "Farm Problem" = unstable prices + incomes

Basic S+D "farm problem" model maintains —

— S is inelastic
— S is random
— D is inelastic
— D is income-inelastic + moves out slowly
— S increases more rapidly than demand.

Gardner gives a very good picture of overall structural issues in agriculture of U.S. — notes many of the issues we have been pointing out —

— increasing off-farm work
— migration of labor out of agriculture
— high farmer wealth + income
— skip over policy discussions — not entirely relevant today.

What causes farm policies to be what they are?

We could have an entire class on this — but we need to at least say a little about policy issues — one of my favorite papers —

Gardner (1987 JPE) — causes of U.S. farm programs

Uses Peltzman-Stigler political economy framework to consider the underlying determinants of U.S farm programs.

Many Questions —

— Why do some farm commodities receive a lot of support (e.g. cotton) and others less or even none (cattle) ?

— Why does protection for some commodities weaken over time + strengthen for others?

Policy involves the redistribution of economic welfare from some groups (taxpayers) to others (producers)

These transfers entail costs = D W Losses + free riders

Politicians use these transfers to garner political support.

Different types of policies generate different types of losses + transfers.

These losses, in turn, depend on elasticities of S + D.

e.g. — consider policy instrument that will use subsidy to guarantee producers a given price (a deficiency payment program) —

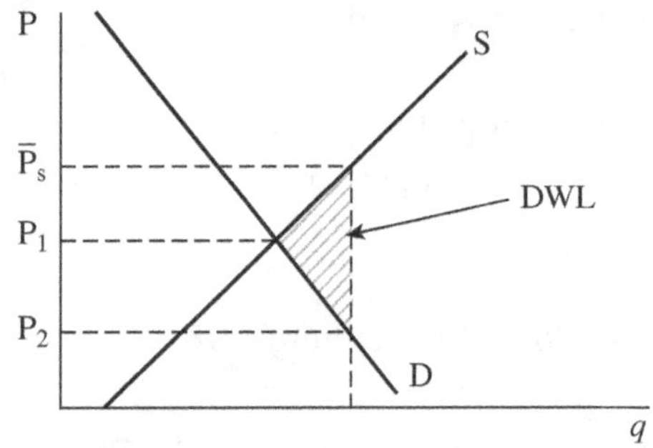

cost of policy = DWL — made bigger by —

— greater elasticity of S
— lower elasticity of D

Thus elasticities should affect DWL and thus affect policy choices

Economic factors + characteristics of a commodity could also reflect demand for support —

— costs of organizing + maintaining lobby effort
- — number of producers
- — spatial dispersion of production
- — concentration of industry
- — variability of production (cost of organizing)

Specific Variables

1) State level index of concentration (Herfindahl)
   - — beef cattle = .004 (very diverse)
   - — sugar cane = 0.46 (very concentrated)
2) Variability of production by state — reflects costs of organization + communication — large when production is shifting in/out of a state
3) Rate of output growth — rapid growth may place obstacles in way of political organization
4) Higher output/produces — increases producers' expected returns to lobbying
5) S + D elasticities — which Gardner estimates
6) Share of commodity exported — higher = more elastic overall demand
7) Share of commodity imported — easy to tax if foreign producers can bear costs
8) Share of land in production costs ⇒ should make S less elastic
9) Livestock production

   Dependent variable = producers' price gains that result from farm programs (as % of price) = $\ln\left(P^D/P^W\right)$

Uses Tobit Model to Estimate — Results

1) Low elastic of S or D ⇒ more intervention
2) Nonlinear effect of groups size — you want to be small — but not too small as to not matter
3) More instability in production ⇒ less support
4) More concentration geographically ⇒ more support
5) Bigger production units (farms) ⇒ more support
6) Imported goods (wool, sugar) get more protection
7) Repeats using subset of commodities with support price.
   — Similar results.

A few issues on estimation of acreage response functions —

1. What price to use? —

Gardner 1976 AJAE — futures prices —

Estimates common specification of acreage response functions —

$$A_t = \alpha + \beta_1 P_t + \beta_2 P_t^s + \beta_3 A_{t-1}$$

Lagged d.v. = partial adjustment — often included on basis of adaptive expectations (Via Nerlove)

Gardner argues in favor of using future price — a planting — time quota for a post-harvest contract (January or December)

Futures price work well and yield slightly more elastic responses.

2. What is the role of risk?

Chavas and Halt 1990 AJAE —

Use expected utility maximization, which implies —

— Volatility of prices and yields may matter
— Wealth may matter (e.g. DARA preferences)
— Government programs may truncate distribution of prices — e.g. price supports (assume normality)

— Use results for moments of truncated random variables to derive effects of government price supports

Estimate models of corn + soybean average response
Aggregate data 1954–85
Equations:

$$A_{it} = a_i + \alpha_i \left(w_{t-1} + \sum_t A_j \bar{\pi}_{jt} \right) + \sum_j \beta_{ij} \tilde{\pi}_{it}$$
$$\sum_{k \geq j} \sum_j \gamma_{ijk} \hat{\sigma}_{jkt} + \theta t + nD83$$

Π_i = profits crop *i*
They find —

— Reasonable price elasticities
— Small risk elasticities — soybeans more responsive to risk than corn
— Reject CARA in favor of DARA

Technology, Structural Change + Innovation

Technological change =

1) More output per unit of input
2) Change in production function parameter

Technological change often favors one or more inputs over others — biased change.

One consideration of technological change involves shifts in isoquant —

— a parallel shift is factor neutral
— a shift may, however, favor one input →

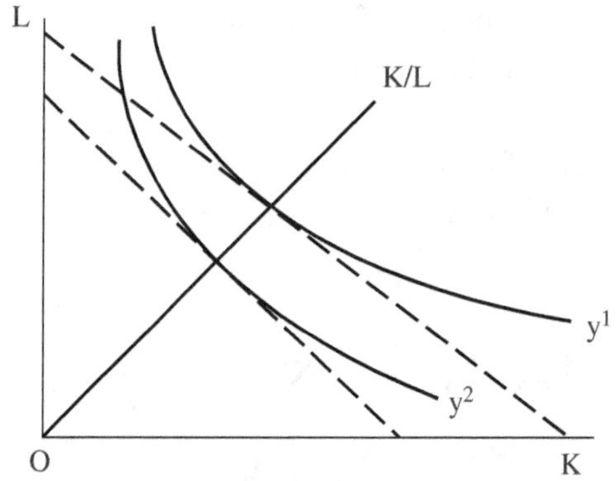

k — saving

3 Measures of Technological Bias

Consider $F_K\, K/F_L\, L$

1) Hicks — measures bias for fixed K/L ratio (as above)
2) Harrod — measure bias along fixed K/Y rartio
3) Solow — measure bias along fixed L/Y ratio

Where does it come from?

Induced innovation = changes in relative prices lead to research and innovation efforts

A Classic Paper on Technological Change

Griliches 1957 Econometrics — Hybrid corn —

Hybrid corn = selectively bred corn with superior attributes for specific areas.

Question — why rapid adoption in some areas + slow in others? Early in some, late in others —

Famous picture —

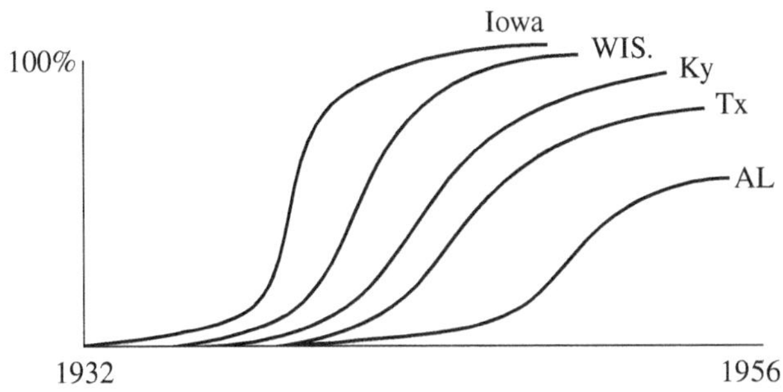

Uses "S-shaped" logistic curve to attempt to represent adoption

$$p = k / 1 + e^{-(a+b\cdot t)}$$

P = % adoption b = rate of adoption
K = ceiling /equilibrium value a = timing of adoption

Griliches uses crops reporting district data to calculate estimates of these curves for different state.

Obtained excellent fit to data.

Adoption started in Corn Belt (defines date of 10% adoption level as "origin of adoption")

Now uses these fitted parameters as variable in analysis of factor that brought about adoption —

1. Origin of adoption —

Relevant variables

Y = date of origin

X_1 = market density = average corn acreage * K/ land in farms

X_3 = scale effect = average corn acreage/ farm

S = slope of logarithmic function

X_4 = "Corn Beltness" = % of corn lines that are accounted for by Corn Belt varieties

X_{10} = earliest date of adoption in neighborhood

Uses simple correlation and regression methods to evaluate.

Dates of origin reflect fact that introduction of hybrid seed accrued according to expected profitability — "better" areas entered first.

2. Rate of acceptance /adoption —

Measured by b = slope of function

Expected to reflect profitability of the adoption

Measures using:

X_7 = average increase in yield
X_8 = long run average pre-hybrid yield
X_3 = average corn acres (scale)

All positively related to adoption

3. Equilibrium level of use (K = ceiling on adoption) used log $(K(1 - K))$

Used X_3 = scale
X_8 = pre-hybrid average yield
X_{11} = value of land and buildings

All positively related

Overall — adoption reflects economic factors —

— Reflects profitability of introducing hybrids by seed companies
— profitability of adoption by farmers

Olmsted and Rhode 1993 JPE —

Was agricultural technical change a result of induced innovation?

Induced innovation — technological change represents a response to market prices.

For a very long time — work of Hayami + Ruttan (1971, 1985) — thought to provide a perfect representation of these for agriculture.

In other sectors, the story has not been so clear — with empirical evidence supporting other explanations.

$H + R$ — considered output/labor
output/land
land/labour } for U. S. + Japan

$H + R$ observed 2 things —

— In *U.S.*, as labor become more expensive, other sources of power (capital) were substituted for labor — land/labor ratio rising

— In Japan, land very scare — expensive — technological progress led to biological advances that raised output per unit of land.

O+R claim evidence does not fit this and that there are errors in the *H–R* story

O+R focus on disaggregating the data on a regional basis — they find that the story changes across regions.

Learning by Doing

Jovanovic and Nyarko (1996 Econometrica) —

— A simple model that characterizes learning through Bayesian updating

Assume risk neutrality —

Agent has several grades of technology to choose from

Grade is indexed by n n(0, ∞) —

Grade reflected in parameter of production function

$$q = \gamma^n [1 - (y_{nt} - Z)^2] \qquad \gamma > 1$$

where $y_{nt} = \theta_n + w_{nt}$

y_{nt} is a random target that fluctuates around θ_n = grade specific parameter with $W_{nt} = N(0,\sigma^2_w)$ variate

Agent does not know θ_n — but has prior beliefs about it

var(θ_n) = posterior variance

Optimal decision and expected output given by —

$$Z = E_t(y_{nt}) = E_t(\theta_n)$$
$$E_t(q) = \gamma^n [1 - var_t(\theta_n) - \sigma^2_w]$$

This second expression suggests posterior precision of θ_n is analogous to an index of human capital.

Switching Technology

Assume no cost to do so —
Assume relationships $\theta_n + \theta_{n+K}$ $K \geq 0$ is

$\theta_{n+K} = \alpha^{k/2}\,\theta_n + e_k$

Where $e_k \sim N(0, \rho_K\,\sigma_e^2)$

$$\rho_k = \begin{cases} (1-\alpha^k)/(1-\alpha) & \text{for } \alpha \neq 1 \\ k & \alpha = 1 \end{cases}$$

α = represents extent that human capital can be transferred across technology —

$\alpha = 0$ — human capital is technology specific
$\alpha = 1$ — human capital is freely transferable

Agent forms prior about θ_n

J + M describe 3 processes for transfer of knowledge —

1) Bayesian updating (within a technology)
2) Transfer of knowledge (to a new technology)
3) Transfer + then updating (combination of (1) + (2))

Describes how prior variance is updated in each case

An Application of Learning by Doing

Foster and Rosenzweig JPE 1995 —

Learning from peers + neighbor plays on important role.

Application is to adoption of HYV: high yield variety rice + wheat seeds in Punjab India

Allow for partial adoption and multiple technologies

Adopt target input model we just described —

$$\tilde{\theta}_{ijt} = \theta^* + u_{ijt}$$

θ^* = mean optimal use of input (fertilizers)
U_{ijt} = iid shock mean = 0, variance = σ_u^2
Farmers know σ_u^2 and have prior on θ^*
Prior $\theta^* \sim M(\hat{\theta}_{j0}, \sigma^2_{\theta j0})$
Yield for traditional varieties is n_a
Yield for *HYV* depends on input use + land quality
According to:

$$\text{Yield HYVith parcel } = n_a + n_n - n_{na}\frac{i}{A_j} - \left(\theta_{ijt} - \bar{\theta}_{ijt}\right)^2$$

Where θ_{ijt} = actual input use
$\bar{\theta}_{ijt}$ = optimal input use
This implies expected profits at t —

$$\Pi_{jt} = \left(n_n - n_{na}\frac{H_{jl}}{2A_j} - \sigma^2_{\theta jt} - \sigma_u^2\right)H_{jt} + n_a A_j + \mu_j + \in_{pjt}$$

H_{jt} = area planted to hybrid
A_j = total area available for cultivation

— The process — farmer plants not knowing optimal input use
— At harvest, the optimal input use in made clear ($\bar{\theta}_{ijt}$)
— Farmer uses this information to update priors
— Information accumulates proportionally with # plots farmer plants to hybrids
— Farmer may also learn from neighbors who also plot *HYV'S*
So, Bayesian updating process is —

$$\sigma^2_{\theta jt} = \frac{1}{\rho + \rho_0 s_{jt} + \rho_v \bar{S}_{-jt}} \{S = \text{vector of exprience}$$

$\rho = 1/\sigma^2_{\theta 0}$ = precision of initial prices
$\rho_0 = 1/\sigma^2_{\mu}$ = precision obtained from each plot (s_{jt}) planted on farmer *j* plot
$\rho_v = n/(\sigma^2_{\mu} + \sigma^2_k)$ = precision gained from plots S_{-jt} planted on neighbors farmers.

Implication

- More cumulative use by farmers and neighbors of hybrids raises their level of future use
- Returns to experience diminish over time

Note — learning is a dynamic problem — involving building experience over time

Agents choose H_j to max —

$$V_{jt} = \max_{H_{jx}} E_t \sum_{x=t}^{T} \delta^{s-t} \Pi_t(\cdot)$$

OR —

$$v_{jt} = \max_{H_{jt}} E_t \left[\left(n_n - n_{na} \frac{H_g}{2A_j} - \sigma_\mu^2 - \frac{1}{\rho + \rho_0 S_{jt} + \rho_v \bar{S}} \right) H_j + n_a A_j + \mu_j + \epsilon_{pjt} \right] + \delta V_{jt+1}$$

FOC's suggest —

$$H_{jt} = h_t\,(s_{jt}, s_{-jt}, A_j, A_{-j})$$

Empirical Analysis

Panel of 4,118 households 1968/65, 69/70, 70/71

Households in 250 villages — can use this to track neighbor's adoption

They find learning by doing + learning from others

HYV use increases with past use and with more use by neighbors

Important learning spillers effects are implied

That is — the growth in experience is accumulated by an individual but also shared across farms

If information was not shared — far lower adoption.

Chapter 11

Asset Values + Rents

$\text{Rents}_t = f(E\text{ (profits)})$

↑Common to decompose into components (payments, market returns, etc.)

Risk of return may also matter since working with uncertain values

In turn — asset values are determined by capitalized/discounted stream of expected future rents —

$$\text{value} = \sum_{t=1}^{\infty} E\left(\frac{Rents_t}{(1+r)^t}\right) + \text{Con}\, v_D$$

↑ conversion option value

How are rental agreements structured?

— Cash (prominent)
— Share
— Hybrid

Cash vs. share — who bears the risk?

Share leases are risk sharing mechanism.

2 relevant papers — Goodwin, Mishra, Ortalo — Magne 2003 + 2011

If is common to decompose rents/returns into individual components.

$$\text{Example} - \Pi_t = \Pi^m{}_t + \Pi^G{}_t$$

↑Market ↑Government Subsidy

And to further decompose these . . .

1996–2014 — Different Programs

1) Fixed direct payments
2) Loan deficiency payments
3) Counter-cyclical (MLA) payments

GMO (2011) consider how these payment affect cash + share rental rates.

Cash → 100% to famers

Share → split

"Buck Stops Where" —

Fixed payments 60–70% claimed by land lord

Share — ≈ 30% LL (measures total $ to famer + land lord)

LDP payment — bigger input on share lease — insurance effect (risk premium)

Models of Land values — an extension —

Common specification

$$LV_t = \beta_i \, E \, \Pi^m{}_{t+1} + \beta_2 \, E\Pi^G{}_{t+1}$$

β_i = discount rate associated with ith source of funds —

What is in β_i?

— price discount rate (riskless asset return)
— expected growth and/or depreciation
— risk of future policy changes

(Note tobacco quota story)

A problem —

Expected (not realized) values drive LV.

In a panel or pooled *ts/cs* data set (commonly used) —

Payments + returns from market VERY correlated in a given year across individual farms — so realized values not good reflection of E_t (value)

Errors in variables problem!

Also significant correlation across errors in a year.

Both papers consider application to ARMS data

— Discuss ARMS

Papers find —

Very different effects from different programs

— Big problem with conventional approach of using realized values as expected
— Results suggest farmers did not expect AMTA to end in 2002
— Different parameters for different years.

Price Transmission

Vertical — Farm ↔ Wholesale ↔ Retail

Horizontal — Market A ↔ Market B

Arbitrage — with transaction costs

Selling $i \rightarrow j - K$ = tran. costs $0 \leq K \leq 1$

Sellers receive $(1-k)P_j$

Implies arbitrage model of —

$$1/(1-K) \geq p_i/p_j \geq (1-K)$$

Or, in log term —

$$-\ln(1-K) \geq (P_i - P_j) \geq \ln(1-K)$$

Implies a neutral band (commodity points)

$$[-\ln(1-K), \ln(1-K)]$$

$$\text{Alternative } -P_i = A.P_j^{B_1}\, T_{ij}^{B_2}\ldots \quad \left.\right\}\begin{matrix}\text{Expect } \beta_i = 1 \\ \forall_i\end{matrix}$$

$$\text{ln logs } P_i = \ln(A) + \beta_1 p_j + \beta_2 t_{ij} + \ldots$$

Widely recognized that nominal prices are nonstationary —

$$P_t = \rho P_{t-1} + \varepsilon_t$$

$|p| < 1 \Rightarrow$ stationary
Test using

$$\Delta Pt = (\rho - 1)\, P_{t-1} + V_t$$

λ
$\uparrow$Test $\lambda = 0$ – *ADF, PP, KPSS, NP…*

When considering linkages — consider cointegration

$$Y_{1t} - \beta_1\, y_{2t} - \ldots - \beta_K\, y_{kt} = V_t$$

V_t = Departure from long run equilibrium

$$V_t = \rho V_{t-1} + e_t$$

Or — in "Error correction form" —

$$\Delta\, V_t - \lambda\, V_{t-1} + e_t$$

T_{say} introduced idea of tests + specification of TAR models —

$$\rho = \begin{cases} \rho_1 & if\,|\,v_{t-1}\,| \le C \\ \rho_2 & if\,|\,v_{t-1}\,| > C \end{cases}$$

C = "Threshold parameter"
Recall E–G representation theorem — any cointegration model can be represented by equivalent VECM —

$$\Delta y_{it} = \sum_j \Gamma_j \Delta y_{ijt} + \beta v_{t-1}$$

$$\vdots$$

$$\Delta y_{kt} = \cdots\cdots\cdots\cdots\cdots\cdots$$

Balke + Fomby extended this to consider TVECM

$$\Delta y_t = \begin{cases} \sum_i \gamma_i^1 \Delta y_{t-i} + \theta^1 V_{t-1} + \varepsilon_t^1 & |V_{t-1}| \leq C \\ \sum_i \gamma_i^2 \Delta y_{t-i} + \theta^2 V_{t-1} + \varepsilon_t^2 & |V_{t-1}| > C \end{cases}$$

Can here multiple regions + multiple thresholds
Testing for Thresholds —
T say – order V_{t-1}, V_t values + use recursive residuals regressed on V_{t-1}

$$\text{Test: } -\gamma_i^1 = \gamma_i^2 \text{ and } \theta^1 = \theta^2$$

Davies problem — Hansen test

Discuss —

— Estimation is grid search
— Simple TVAR of price differential —

Define $Y_t = P_t^1 - P_t^2$
Consider $\Delta y_t = \lambda y_{t-1}$
$\lambda = 0 \Rightarrow$ price differential is nonstationary
ln (.5) /ln $(1+\lambda)$ = denotes half–life
should see $-1 < \lambda < 0$ for error correction to devise
Impulses – *IF*
GIF
Also used to examine asymmetric in adjustments
Why might we see thresholds + asymmetric adjustment?

www.ingramcontent.com/pod-product-compliance
Lightning Source LLC
La Vergne TN
LVHW020234210926
848481LV00016B/1969